Pioneers and Explorers in North America

Pioneers and Explorers in North America

Summaries of Biographical Articles in History Journals

People in History Series

Pamela R. Byrne and
Susan K. Kinnell, Editors

ABC-CLIO

Santa Barbara, California
Oxford, England

Cover design by Tanya Nigh
Book design by Susan K. Kinnell

Library of Congress Cataloging in Publication Data

Pioneers and explorers in North America.

      (The People in history series)
      Includes indexes.
      1. Explorers—North America—Biography. 2. Pioneers—North America—Biography. I. Byrne, Pamela R.
  II. Kinnell, Susan K. III. Series.
E36.P56 1988   970'.009'92 [B]   88-6201
ISBN 0-87436-540-6 (pbk.)

10 9 8 7 6 5 4 3 2 1

ABC-Clio, Inc.
2040 Alameda Padre Serra, Box 4397
Santa Barbara, California 93103

Clio Press Ltd.
55 St. Thomas Street
Oxford, OX1 1JG, England

This book is printed on acid-free paper ∞.
Manufactured in the United States of America.

CONTENTS

PREFACE

This is a book about people — specifically, pioneers and explorers in North America. Not every one that you can think of is in this book, nor is every important thing mentioned about the pioneers who are included. *PIONEERS AND EXPLORERS IN NORTH AMERICA* has 226 summaries of articles about US and Canadian trappers, mountainmen, Indians, wagon train pioneers, and surveyors, among others. There are many unknown pioneers and explorers as as well as famous ones — from John Jacob Astor's fur empire and Daniel Boone to Alice McDonald, a cook in Alaskan mining camps.

Using this volume, students can select topics for term papers and identify the names of specific pioneers they wish to research further. Fictional or composite characters can be created by reading about several people doing the same kind of work or living in the same time and place. Role enactment in the classroom will be greatly enhanced by access to the people described in these summaries. Groups of pioneers in history (such as gold rush miners) can be studied from several different perspectives, providing the teacher and the student with new approaches to learning.

PIONEERS AND EXPLORERS IN NORTH AMERICA differs from standard biographical dictionaries, which usually provide information about well-known people. Instead, this book brings to the reader's attention some of the lesser-known and the almost unknown pioneers in American history in addition to a sampling of the famous ones. The chronological scope of the summaries ranges from the seventeenth century to the present, and the lives touched upon are those of individuals who have been the subjects of historians' research in the many journals covered in *America: History and Life*. The stories of these independent people will give a sense of the richness and diversity of everyday life at various times, providing a dimension to the study of history that is often missing in textbooks.

The entries in this book are summaries of some of the articles that have appeared over the years in thousands of history journals and that were selected by the editors at ABC-CLIO. It is to be hoped that the inclusion of varying sources (the journal literature from which these articles and summaries were taken) will direct students toward new avenues of research and help them consider new sources of information outside the realm of their usual classroom and library study. The list of journals covered in this book contains a number of titles that will be familiar to secondary school teachers and librarians and several that they may not previously have considered as a source for curriculum-based research. Interlibrary loans should provide access to these more unfamiliar journals so that further exploration and research may be carried out.

A NOTE ON HOW TO USE THIS BOOK:

The summaries are arranged alphabetically by the names of the pioneers. A detailed subject index allows the student to find people by region, occupation, ethnic origin, or other unique factors. (See the note at the beginning of the index for a discussion on how to use this index.) All summaries and their original articles are in English. If there is more than one article about a particular person, the articles will appear alphabetically by the author of the article. If the original article had no author, the article is listed with the title first. A list of the article authors and the periodicals covered follows the subject index. A sample entry appears on the following page.

SAMPLE ENTRY

Name of Person

Entry Number   Article Author

KITCHEN, PETER

Article Title

104.   Snoke, Elizabeth R.   PETE KITCHEN:
ARIZONA PIONEER.
Arizona and the West 1979 21 (3): 235-256.

Journal
Information

Peter Kitchen (1819-95) was the epitome of a
successful pioneer who gave stability to the
southwest frontier.   He arrived in Arizona in
1854 and established himself in cattle and
farming.   He developed a profitable business
supplying meat, grain, and vegetables to southern
Arizona communities, mines, and military posts.
He bought and sold interests in local mines.
Kitchen moved to Tucson in 1883 to spend the
rest of his life in real estate, gambling, and civic
events.   He has become a legendary frontier folk
hero.

Summary

PIONEERS AND EXPLORERS IN NORTH AMERICA

A
___

ADAMS, ANDY

1. Johnson, Carole M. A DEDICATION TO THE MEMORY OF ANDY ADAMS, 1859-1935.
Arizona and the West 1977 19(3): 202-206.

Indiana-born Andy Adams (1859-1935) spent the 1880's and 1890's in the cattle industry and mining in the Great Plains and Southwest. When an 1898 play's portrayal of Texans outraged him, he started writing plays, short stories, and novels drawn from his own experiences. His *The Log of a Cowboy* became a classic novel about the cattle business, especially the cattle drive. No other production from this inveterate writer could match it, and his later efforts were increasingly rejected by publishers. His works are acclaimed and criticized for their fidelity to truth and their lack of literary qualities.

ADAMSON, SARAH BROWNE ARMSTRONG

2. Riley, Glenda and Benning, Carol. THE 1836-1845 DIARY OF SARAH BROWNE ARMSTRONG ADAMSON OF FAYETTE COUNTY, OHIO.
Old Northwest 1984 10(3): 285-306.

Discusses the life of Sarah Browne Armstrong Adamson (1783-1851) and her diary, which gives a detailed account of her family's economic, social, and personal activities on their Fayette County, Ohio, farm. Selections from the diary, including poetry, offer insights into the primary interests and concerns of a farm woman and her family on the farm frontier in the mid-19th century.

AGUIRRE, MARTIN

3. Hoffman, Abraham. THE CONTROVERSIAL CAREER OF MARTIN AGUIRRE: THE RISE AND FALL OF A CHICANO LAWMAN.
California History 1984 63(4): 293-304, 339-341.

Traces the law enforcement career of Martin Aguirre. A native Californio, Aguirre acquired early fame when he rescued 19 people from the Los Angeles River in a January 1886 rainstorm. He served as sheriff of Los Angeles County, 1888-90, losing a reelection bid in a hotly contested election. His loyalty to the Republican Party won him an appointment as warden of San Quentin Prison in 1899, but his term was marred by accusations of political favoritism and graft. Thereafter he served as a deputy sheriff and bailiff in Los Angeles County until his death in 1929.

AIROLA, MANUEL

4. Burrows, Jack. THE GREATEST BRONC BUSTER WHO EVER LIVED.
Am. West 1983 20(3): 54-58.

Manuel Airola (1888-1925) was "the archetypal cowboy whose Homeric exploits on bucking broncs" is a legend still remembered in the hill country of northern California. "Manny" or "Mandy" defied danger, sustained repeated broken bones and injuries, won numerous prizes, and earned the awe and respect of rodeo audiences.

AKROFF, GEORGE

5. Ursenbach, Charles. THE GREAT CROWSNEST PASS TRAIN HOLDUP.
Alberta Hist. .(Canada) 1984 32(2): 1-8.

Three men from Great Falls, Montana, George Akroff, Tom Bassoff, and Alex Areloff (or Auloff), held up a train at Crowsnest Pass, Alberta, 7 August 1920. Five days later a gun battle resulted in the death of Areloff while Akroff and Bassoff, though wounded, escaped. Two policemen were also killed. An extensive manhunt ensued that on 11 August resulted in the arrest of Bassoff, then 31 years of age. He received a two-day trial in October, and death by hanging on 22 December 1920. Akroff was eventually tracked down in Portland, Washington, and was returned to Canada where he died after serving only three years of his seven-year prison sentence.

ALLEN, ETHAN

6. Linscott, Elizabeth. ETHAN ALLEN: SOLDIER, ORATOR, AUTHOR.
New-England Galaxy 1977 19(2): 49-56.

Describes the roles played by Ethan Allen in the settlement of Vermont, in its development as an independent republic, and in the American Revolution. Highlights his capture of Fort Ticonderoga, his capture by the British at Montreal, and his captivity in England.

7. Sabine, David B. ETHAN ALLEN AND THE GREEN MOUNTAIN BOYS.
Am. Hist. Illus. 1977 11(9): 8-15.

Gives an account of the life of Ethan Allen and the establishment of the Green Mountain Boys, and their part in the American Revolution, especially the capture of Fort Ticonderoga in 1775.

ANDERSON, JAMES WALLACE (FAMILY)

8. Anderson, George M. AN EARLY COMMUTER: THE LETTERS OF JAMES AND MARY ANDERSON.
Maryland Hist. Mag. 1980 75(3): 217-232.

James Wallace Anderson (1797-1881) and Mary, his wife, owned a farm called Vallombrosa in Montgomery County, two miles north of Rockville, Maryland. Working as an auditor in the US Post Office in Washington, D.C., 1854-61, James was able to go home only twice a month or so, and thus carried on a frequent correspondence with his wife. Their 400 or so letters, here discussed and quoted by their great-grandson, provide an unusually full picture of urban boarding house life in the capital and rural farm existence in the mid-19th century. Brief biographical details of the couple's eight children are also included, along with the history of the farm to 1960.

ANDERSON, JOSEPH RICHARD "SKOOKUM JOE"

9. Mueller, George D. REAL AND FANCIED CLAIMS: JOSEPH RICHARD "SKOOKUM JOE" ANDERSON, MINER IN CENTRAL MONTANA, 1880-1897.
Montana 1985 35(2): 50-59.

Joseph Richard "Skookum Joe" Anderson was a legendary prospector in central Montana. Stories abound of his exploits in the Northwest, Utah, and California before he settled in Montana, where he discovered several rich veins of gold. Between 1886 and 1895 "Skookum Joe" recorded his activities in diaries by which we can measure the legendary prospector against the real life miner. Joe was a hard-working prospector who knew his business, made valuable gold discoveries, and organized their exploitation. He was not the isolated prospector of legend; rather, he was a friendly man with great curiosity about the outside world.

ANDERSON, ROBERT BALL

10. Wax, Darold D. ROBERT BALL ANDERSON, A KENTUCKY SLAVE, 1843-1864.
Register of the Kentucky Hist. Soc. 1983 81(3): 255-273.

Born to a slave woman on 1 March 1843, Robert Ball Anderson lived to the age of 87 and achieved a substantial fortune in land and livestock in western Nebraska. Anderson's Greene County Kentucky owner considered him a favorite and recognized his qualities, but conflicts with the owner's wife led to his transfer to field work in 1859. In late 1864, Anderson left the plantation and joined the Union army. In 1870, he acquired 80 acres of land in Nebraska through the Homestead Act, and, after some initial difficulties, success and wealth came to him in the Nebraska panhandle.

11. Wax, Darold D. ROBERT BALL ANDERSON, EX-SLAVE, A PIONEER IN WESTERN NEBRASKA, 1884-1930.
Nebraska Hist. 1983 64(2): 163-192.

Robert Ball Anderson, a slave born in Kentucky on 1 March 1843, joined the Union army in the fall of 1864 and served in the 125th Colored Infantry. After the Civil War, Anderson worked as a farmer and farmhand in Nebraska and Kansas. In 1884, he filed a claim under the Timber Culture Act near Hemingford in the Nebraska Sandhills. Anderson's small farm prospered and grew, and by 1910 he was a widely respected citizen and the largest black landowner in Nebraska. His autobiography, published in 1927, relates primarily Anderson's experiences as a slave in Kentucky.

12. Wax, Darold D. THE ODYSSEY OF AN EX-SLAVE: ROBERT BALL ANDERSON'S PURSUIT OF THE AMERICAN DREAM.
Phylon 1984 45(1): 67-79.

Discusses the life of Robert Ball Anderson from the time he escaped slavery to join the Union Army in 1864, until his decision to settle in Nebraska in 1884. This decision took many years to materialize, but at his death in 1930, Anderson was the largest black landowner in Nebraska.

ANTISARLOOK, MARY

13. Ray, Dorothy Jean. SINROCK MARY: FROM ESKIMO WIFE TO REINDEER QUEEN.
Pacific Northwest Quarterly 1984 75(3): 98-107.

Sheldon Jackson, Presbyterian missionary and first general agent of education for Alaska, imported a domesticated reindeer herd from Russia to Alaska in 1892 to provide a new industry for Eskimos. He initiated the experiment on the Sinuk River and placed the herd under the supervision of Charlie and Mary Antisarlook. Under their careful management the herd increased, but Charlie's death in 1900 sparked a legal battle with his relatives who wished to take control of the herd from Mary. Her courtroom victory was expensive, but Mary emerged with full control of the reindeer. Prior to her death in 1948, Mary had become a legend because of her generosity toward other Eskimos and her adoption of eleven Eskimo children.

ASTOR, JOHN JACOB

14. Humins, John H. FURS, ASTOR AND INDIANS. *Michigan History 1985 69(2): 24-31.*

John Jacob Astor founded a fur empire, aided by friendly politicians and the federal government. The end result was that both white and Indian traders became indebted to Astor. Subsequently, these debts helped convince the Indians to accept the treaties offered by the US government, bringing great quantities of land into the public domain and making Astor an extemely wealthy man.

ATWOOD, HENRY STILES

15. Brooks, Daniel Fate. HENRY STILES ATWOOD: ANTEBELLUM ECCENTRIC OF WILCOX COUNTY. *Alabama Rev. 1981 34(1): 20-30.*

Examines the migration of both Northerners and Southerners, and, in particular, that of Henry Stiles Atwood to Wilcox County, Alabama, during the first quarter of the 19th century. Atwood, who purchased land in the county in 1821, established himself as a very energetic merchant. His business success provided him with the revenue to buy vast landholdings and a large number of slaves. His eccentric ways, secretiveness, reputation as a "rainmaker," and devotion to the anti-masonic movement were culminated in his "strange will," which charged his executors with providing educational opportunities and monetary support for his seven mulatto children.

AVERY, WILLIAM WAIGHTSTILL

16. Gass, W. Conard. THE MISFORTUNE OF A HIGH MINDED AND HONORABLE GENTLEMAN: W. W. AVERY AND THE SOUTHERN CODE OF HONOR. *North Carolina Hist. Rev. 1979 56(3): 278-297.*

On Tuesday, 11 November 1851, William Waightstill Avery (1816-64), a lawyer, shot and killed Samuel Flemming (b. 1812), a businessman and politician, in the Burke County courthouse at Morganton, North Carolina. Three weeks earlier Flemming had cowhided and beaten an unarmed and surprised

Avery on the main street of Marion, North Carolina, culminating their several years of political, legal, and personal disputes. Avery, of an upper class North Carolina family, felt he had to kill Flemming to retain his standing according to the southern gentleman's code of honor. Tried immediately after the killing, Avery was acquitted by a jury which believed so firmly in that code that it was willing to overlook outright murder to uphold it.

B

BACA, FELIPE

17. Baca, Luis and Baca, Facundo. HISPANIC PIONEER: DON FELIPE BACA BRINGS HIS FAMILY NORTH TO TRINIDAD.
Colorado Heritage 1982 (1): 26-35.

Don Felipe Baca (1829-74) and 12 other Hispano families moved from New Mexico in 1862 to the area of Trinidad, Colorado. He was active in Colorado territorial politics and was a large sheep producer. Two of his sons, Luis (an engineer) and Facundo (a physician) left personal narratives of their father, excerpts from which are included. Also included is a comment in Spanish made "in an Albuquerque Spanish-language newspaper" on Felipe's wife, Maria Gonzales Baca. The Baca adobe house is now a regional museum operated by the Colorado Historical Society.

BAKER, EDGAR CROW

18. Brooks, G. W. S. EDGAR CROW BAKER: AN ENTREPRENEUR IN EARLY BRITISH COLUMBIA.
BC Studies (Canada) 1976 (31): 23-43.

Edgar Crow Baker (d. 1920) was a representative entrepreneur in Victoria when that city was the social, business, and political center of British Columbia. Although he came to Victoria as an employee, he had ideas and ambitions, a valuable family connection, and fraternal affiliations that allowed him into the business life of the city. Baker was involved in almost every major economic activity in the province: land, lumber, railroads, coal, shipping, public utilities. He was also active in municipal, provincial, and federal politics.

BAKER, JOHN W. B.

19. Baker, John W. B. INTO THE NORTH.
Alberta History (Canada) 1985 33(2): 19-27.

As a pioneer resident of the Peace River area in Alberta during the last great days of fur trading, John W. B. Baker addressed the opening of the Fort St. John Museum in February 1984 by recounting his life in the Canadian North during 1928-48. He describes the topography, Eskimo life, animal life, trade under the jurisdiction of the Hudson's Bay Company, and key individuals—bush pilots, missionaries—in this geographical area, and discusses his careers as a radio operator at Watson Lake, and later as a chief dispatcher for Canadian Pacific Air Lines.

BARNARD, GEORGE

20. Willingham, John. GEORGE BARNARD: TRADER AND MERCHANT ON THE TEXAS FRONTIER.
Texana 1973 12(4): 305-334.

In the late 1830's George Barnard came to the Waco, Texas region from Hartford, Connecticut. Only 19 years of age at the time, he was the first white settler in the region. Becoming resident agent there at a post established by the firm of John F. Torrey and Brothers of Houston, he traded with the area Indians and invested heavily in land. By 1857 he was financially secure and went into semi-retirement, dying in 1883.

BARNEY, JOSHUA

21. Levin, Alexandra Lee. HOW COMMODORE JOSHUA BARNEY OUTWITTED THE BRITISH AT NORFOLK.
Maryland Hist. Mag. 1978 73(2): 163-167.

Summarizes the colorful career of the "Prince of privateers and adventurers," Commodore Joshua Barney (1759-1818), ardent Francophile, who in August, 1797 was blockaded in Norfolk by a British squadron seeking to intercept the two French frigates commanded by Barney with supplies for St. Domingo. Executing "one of his most brilliant feats of seamanship," Barney gave the British the slip by hiding behind a point on the Eastern Shore and making Vice-Admiral Vandeput think he'd gone to sea the previous night. Barney's service to the nation during the war of 1812 while commanding the *Rossie,* and his flight at Bladensburg caused the citizenry of the Chesapeake region to cease holding his service in the French navy against him.

BARRY, KATE

22. Miller, Mary Montgomery. KATE BARRY. *Daughters of the American Revolution Magazine 1984 118(9): 644-646.*

Recounts the life of Kate Barry and her exploits as a volunteer scout for the Patriot forces in South Carolina during the American Revolution.

BARTRAM, JOHN AND WILLIAM

23. Kastner, Joseph. COLONIAL BOTANIST, SELF-TAUGHT, FILLED EUROPEAN GARDENS. *Smithsonian 1977 8(7): 122-129.*

John Bartram (1699-1777), American farmer and self-taught botanist working out of Philadelphia, systematically collected and shipped plant specimens through his primary contact Peter Collinson in London, to the highest levels of European society avid for new plants. During four decades he introduced nearly one-third of the 600 American plants then known in Europe. Appointed King's botanist in 1765, he explored the Carolinas, Georgia, and Florida, opening untouched regions to the study of natural history.

24. Merritt, J. I., III. WILLIAM BARTRAM IN AMERICA'S EDEN. *Hist. Today (Great Britain) 1978 28(11): 712-721.*

Brief biography of American botanist and explorer William Bartram (1739-1823), detailing his explorations in the American South.

BASS, SAM

25.   Robbins, Peggy.   SAM BASS: THE TEXAS ROBIN HOOD.
Am. Hist. Illus. 1982 17(4): 37.

Brief biography of the short-lived cowboy and bandit, Sam Bass, who became known as "the Texas Robin Hood" because he paid poor folks for various services and friendly gestures with gold pieces he had stolen.

BEALE, EDWARD FITZGERALD

26.   Thompson, Gerald.   EDWARD FITZGERALD BEALE AND THE CALIFORNIA GOLD RUSH, 1848-1850.
Southern California Q. 1981 63(3): 198-225.

Traces the movement and activities of Edward Fitzgerald Beale (1822-1903). Having served as an acting naval lieutenant with distinction in the Mexican War, Beale traveled across Mexico with official reports on the discovery of gold in California. He won fame in Washington, D. C., as word spread of his perilous trip and the news he brought. Beale traveled back and forth between California and the East several times between 1848 and 1850. He found time to marry, shared the excitement of the gold rush with his friend John C. Fremont, and guided journalist Bayard Taylor around the gold fields. Beale also brought east a copy of California's new state Constitution. Not yet 30 years old, by 1850 Beale had become a well-known figure on the verge of a long and successful career.

BECKER, CHRISTIAN C.

27.   Iseminger, Gordon L.   C. C. BECKER: MCINTOSH COUNTY GERMAN-RUSSIAN PIONEER.
North Dakota Hist. 1983 50(3): 4-13.

Describes the experiences on the Dakota frontier of Christian C. Becker, one of the German-Russian pioneers who settled the area in the late 1800's. Settling soon after McIntosh County was opened in 1884, Becker and his family faced the hardships of droughts, prairie fires, and blizzards common for frontier farmers. Establishing himself as a farmer, Becker was a leader in forming a school for the immigrant children, in establishing the Zion Lutheran Church, and in establishing the new political structure of the community.

BELL, MONTGOMERY

28. MONTGOMERY BELL AND THE NARROWS OF HARPETH.
Tennessee Hist. Q. 1976 35(1): 3-28.

Outlines the career of Dickson County ironmaker Montgomery Bell (1769-1855). Called Tennessee's first industrialist, Bell practiced his art from its beginnings to its emergence as a major industry. The tunnel that he completed at the Narrows of Harpeth before 1820, now listed in the *National Register of Historic Places* , is an engineering masterpiece and possibly the oldest extant tunnel in the United States. Bell built his Patterson Forge ironworks at the narrows after attempting for a decade to sell his land to the federal government for an armory.

BENGE, BOB

29. Evans, E. Raymond. NOTABLE PERSONS IN CHEROKEE HISTORY: BOB BENGE.
J. of Cherokee Studies 1976 1(2): 98-106.

Bob Benge, a mixed-blood Cherokee leader, was born about 1760. He was extremely anti-American and led many forays against the Americans after the Revolution. He gained a considerable reputation among both Indians and whites for his exploits. Most of his career was military, and in Tennessee and Virginia. Benge, a relative of Sequoyah, was killed in ambush by a Virginia militia officer named Hobbs on 9 April 1794.

BENJAMIN, SARAH MARY

30. Eldred, Richard O. THE HEROINE OF YORKTOWN. *Daughters of the American Revolution Magazine 1984 118(9): 634-636, 698.*

Sarah Mary Benjamin followed her second husband, Aaron Osborn, as he served in Washington's army in the American Revolution and witnessed the British surrender at Yorktown; she later moved to Mount Pleasant Township, Wayne County, Pennsylvania, where she lived to be over 100 and became famous as one of the last survivors of the war.

BENSE, JOHANN

31. Bense, Johann; Doblin, Helga B., transl.; Lynn, Mary C., intro. A BRUNSWICK GRENADIER WITH BURGOYNE: THE JOURNAL OF JOHANN BENSE, 1776-1783. *New York History 1985 66(4): 420-444.*

Although most of the German troops hired by England during the Revolutionary War were Hessians, some 4,000 were from Brunswick. One of the latter, an enlisted man named Johann Bense, kept a journal covering his service from his departure from home early in 1776 to his return in May of 1783. During that time he fought in Burgoyne's army, was captured in late 1777, and spent the remainder of the war as a prisoner. The journal, on microfilm in the Library of Congress for over a half-century, was recently translated and is reprinted here. It is sketchy but reveals a great deal about the life of a hired enlisted soldier during those years.

BENTLEY, WILLIAM

32. Farnam, Anne. DR. BENTLEY'S ACCOUNT BOOKS: DOCUMENTATION FOR THE CREATION OF A HISTORICAL SETTING. *Essex Inst. Hist. Collections 1980 116(4): 206-222.*

The ignored account books of the Reverend William Bentley of Salem, 1783-1819, juxtaposed with his diary, provide new insights into Bentley's daily life. While a boarder from 1791 to 1819 at Hannah Crowninshield's house, now a part of the Essex

Institute, Bentley participated in the remodeling of the house in 1794. His account books detail his involvement. They also contain a 1794 inventory in which he categorized all his possessions, clothing, and books. This allows us to archaeologically reconstruct his living quarters. Includes a well-indexed and annotated copy of this inventory.

BERNAL, JUAN PABLO

33. Delgado, James P. JUAN PABLO BERNAL: CALIFORNIA PIONEER.
Pacific Hist. 1979 23(3): 50-62.

Discusses Juan Pablo Bernal (1810-78), whose family had come to California in the early period of Spanish rule. Born in San Jose de Guadalupe, he saw the territory pass to Mexican rule in 1822, his father obtaining a Mexican land grant. Increase in wealth through cattle breeding on his ranch and successful business transactions in Pueblo de San Jose in addition to his original El Rancho de Santa Teresa made possible his gaining title to El Valle de San Jose in partnership with others of his family. In 1846 the area fell to its American conquerors. After legal battles to maintain titles with American authorities, and bad business deals, he lost much of his wealth. In 1877, one year before his death, he was interviewed at the request of Hubert Howe Bancroft to get material for his *History of California.*

BETHUNE, ANGUS

34. Russell, Hilary. ANGUS BETHUNE.
Judd, Carol M. and Ray, Arthur J., ed.
Old Trails and New Directions: Papers of the Third North American Fur Trade Conference (Toronto: U. of Toronto Pr., 1980): 177-190.

Investigates the career of Angus Bethune (1783-1858) one of the members of the North West Company of Canada who joined the Hudson's Bay Company in 1821. As a Nor'Wester, he was involved in the takeover of Astoria, the company's adventure to China between 1814 and 1816, the "rebellion" of the wintering partners, and the negotiations which led to the coalition of 1821. His career in the Hudson's Bay Company was less dramatic. As a chief factor in the southern department, he clashed with

Governor William Williams and other governmental and company officials. His career was not crowned by many personal successes despite his rank. Nevertheless, his failures influenced the course of the fur trade.

BIDWELL, ANNIE ELLICOTT KENNEDY

35. Mathes, Valerie Sherer. INDIAN PHILANTHROPY IN CALIFORNIA: ANNIE BIDWELL AND THE MECHOOPDA INDIANS.
Arizona and the West 1983 25(2): 153-166.

Using her own family resources and acting on her own initiative, Annie Ellicott Kennedy Bidwell worked with a small band of California Mechoopda Indians to "civilize" them. Encouragd by her wealthy California rancher and congressman husband, she worked closely with the Mechoopda, provided them a school and a church, and supported them financially almost from her marriage in 1868 to her death.

BINGHAM, HIRAM

36. Miller, Char. THE MAKING OF A MISSIONARY: HIRAM BINGHAM'S ODYSSEY.
Hawaiian J. of Hist. 1979 13: 36-45.

Examines Hiram Bingham's early life in Vermont before he sailed for Hawaii in 1819. Age 21 was a turning point for Bingham (1789-1869), because at that time he was to become his parents' caretaker. Instead, he publicly took the vows of the Lord. His conversion to Congregationalism gave him an excuse to break his commitment to his parents. This decision was due largely but not solely to his ambition. Bingham was raised in a religion that demanded intense commitment that went beyond family ties. The demands of his forceful and uncompromising personality fit the requirements of his missionary vocation.

37. Bingham, Afred M. SYBIL'S BONES, A CHRONICLE OF THE THREE HIRAM BINGHAMS.
Hawaiian J. of Hist. 1975 9: 3-36.

Traces the lives of two generations of Binghams. The first Hiram Bingham and his wife Sybil were the models for James

Michener's missionary sequence in his novel *Hawaii* . He made free use of the first Hiram Bingham's *A Residence of Twenty-one Years in the Sandwich Islands* . In later years the Binghams returned to New England, and were dismissed by the American Board of Commissioners for Foreign Missions. The second Hiram Bingham spent his missionary years in the Gilbert Islands until ill health forced his return to Hawaii. The third Hiram Bingham, the author's father, was responsible for moving the bones of Sybil, the first Hiram's first wife, into a grave next to her husband.

BOONE, DANIEL

38. Bloom, Jo Tice. DANIEL BOONE: TRAILBLAZER TO A NATION.
Gateway Heritage 1985 5(4): 28-39.

Long before his death, Daniel Boone was the subject of American frontier legends that, whatever their exaggerations, contributed to building national unity and pride in America. Furthermore, Boone's real achievements, such as his leadership in western trailblazing, remain historical legacies that Boone mythologies can never obscure.

39. DANIEL BOONE: THE FORMATIVE YEARS.
Pennsylvania Heritage 1985 11(1): 34-37.

Traces the history of the Boone family from their immigration to Pennsylvania in 1717 until 1773, when the young Daniel Boone left the colony to settle in the Kentucky wilderness.

BOONE, NATHAN

40. Walker, Wayne T. NATHAN BOONE: THE FORGOTTEN HERO OF MISSOURI.
J. of the West 1979 18(2): 85-94.

Nathan Boone (1781-1856), youngest son of Kentucky pioneer Daniel Boone, settled on his father's Spanish land grant within the Louisiana Territory in 1799. The Boone family's holdings were located in what is now Missouri, near Femme Osage Creek. After the United States purchased the Louisiana Territory, Nathan Boone became a surveyor, guide, and captain of the Missouri Mounted Rangers. Boone served on many military expeditions in several western states between 1812 and 1853; then he retired from the Army as a Lieutenant Colonel.

BRAINERD, DAVID

41. Conforti, Joseph. DAVID BRAINERD AND THE NINETEENTH CENTURY MISSIONARY MOVEMENT. *Journal of the Early Republic 1985 5(3): 309-329.*

Despite a tragically short life marked by illness, personal loss, and repeated disappointment, the Connecticut evangelical minister David Brainerd became a revered figure among early 19th-century evangelical missionaries. Thanks to Jonathan Edwards's extremely popular and highly romanticized *Life of Brainerd* (1748), Brainerd's meager missionary achievements took on heroic proportions. Missionary groups looking for a new role model found inspiration in Brainerd's work among Eastern Indian tribes and discovered the revivalist-pietist impact of the First Great Awakening. An outgrowth of Brainerd's popular appeal was the emphasis Edwards placed on disinterested benevolence and regeneration. Although disinterested benevolence fired missionary zeal, it could not overcome ethnocentrism and selfish attention to personal conversion. In Edwards's hands, Brainerd's life resembled a Puritan devotional work, and it provided a model for 19th-century missionary memoirs.

BRUNSON, ALFRED

42. Schulte, Steven C. ALFRED BRUNSON AND THE WISCONSIN MISSIONARY FRONTIER. *Methodist Hist. 1981 19(4): 231-237.*

Alfred Brunson became a Methodist preacher in 1810. After serving in the War of 1812, he started to ride a circuit in western Pennsylvania and Ohio. In 1835 he proposed that the church found an Indian mission in Wisconsin. Brunson accepted the invitation to become one of the missionaries. He helped in many ways to help build the American Methodist Church and to carry civilization into the wildernesses of the United States.

BYINGTON, CYRUS

43. Coleman, Louis. CYRUS BYINGTON: MISSIONARY TO THE CHOCTAWS.
Chronicles of Oklahoma 1984-85 62(4): 360-387.

Despite his training as a lawyer, Cyrus Byington became a fervent missionary for the American Board of Commissioners for Foreign Missions during 1820. He first served the Choctaw Indians at Mayhew Mission in central Mississippi, and then accompanied them to their new home in southeastern Oklahoma in 1835. In addition to ministering to the Indians, Byington wrote a Choctaw hymnal, grammar, and dictionary, all noted for their accuracy and comprehensiveness. His poor health and Choctaw factionalism during the Civil War troubled Byington's later years, but he remained at his post almost to the time of his death.

BYRD, WILLIAM

44. Greenberg, Michael. WILLIAM BYRD II AND THE WORLD OF THE MARKET.
Southern Studies 1977 16(4): 429-456.

Presents the values, experiences, and aspirations of one of the dominant personalities in colonial Virginia, William Byrd II (1674-1744). He spent most of his time in Virginia directing his economic activities, but closely corresponded with friends in England concerning economic, political, and special conditions there. He had a high opinion of himself and the American aristocracy. He envisaged the establishment of a fully developed market society in America, which would make possible a truly civilized existence and sustain social subordination and consequently slavery, about which he was otherwise uneasy.

C

CALF SHIRT

45. Dempsey, Hugh A. THE SNAKE MAN.
Alberta Hist. (Canada) 1981 29(4): 1-5.

Calf Shirt (1844-1901), of the Many Tumors band of Blackfoot Indians (Blood), had a strange power that permitted him to talk to rattlesnakes. He presented himself as a paradox in his roles as informer and tribal leader, as well as police scout and criminal. In 1888 he formed a new band called the Crooked Backs, which settled near Lethbridge, Alberta. His exploits with snakes resulted in him being featured in numerous shows, including the Territorial Exhibition in Regina in 1895.

CAMPBELL, ARTHUR

46. Hagy, James William. ARTHUR CAMPBELL AND THE WEST, 1743-1811.
Virginia Mag. of Hist. and Biog. 1982 90(4): 456-471.

Traces the career of Arthur Campbell of Washington County. An ambitious man, he helped shape the military and political policies of the state of Virginia, but his stubborn personality prevented his achieving the power and fame he desired. During the 1770's and 1780's, Campbell, as county lieutenant, was instrumental in ridding the western frontier of both Indians and Tories, but he was unwilling to send his militia east to fight the British. Later, Campbell was active in unsuccessful separatist movements that would have made new states from portions of southwestern and western Virginia, North Carolina, and Kentucky.

CAMPBELL, JOHN

47. Hartlen, John. JOHN CAMPBELL: A TRUE PROSPECTOR AND A GOOD GEOLOGIST.
Nova Scotia Hist. Q. (Canada) 1979 9(4): 319-334.

John Campbell, a placer prospector, reported to the legislature that he found gold at Fort Clarence at Halifax Harbour, Nova Scotia, in 1857. In 1861, he extended his efforts to the Sable Island area and discovered gold in the sand and gravel near the island; he also prospected in eastern Nova Scotia. His discoveries had a heavy impact on Nova Scotia's early gold mining industry.

CHOUTEAU, PIERRE

48. Foley, William E. and Rice, Charles David. PIERRE
CHOUTEAU: ENTREPRENEUR AS INDIAN AGENT.
Missouri Hist. Rev. 1978 72(4): 365-387.

Pierre Chouteau, a fur trader and first Indian agent in Upper
Louisiana Territory during 1804-18, is portrayed as a man
striving to handle complex Indian-White relations developing
during the westward movement particularly among the Osage
Indians.

49. Foley, William E. THE LEWIS AND CLARK
EXPEDITION'S SILENT PARTNERS: THE CHOUTEAU
BROTHERS OF ST. LOUIS.
Missouri Hist. Rev. 1983 77(2): 131-146.

Examines the career of Auguste and Pierre Chouteau as
advisers, outfitters, and behind-the-scenes facilitators of the
Lewis and Clark expedition. Pierre became the first Indian
agent, and in this capacity he took two groups of Osage Indians
to Washington to meet government officials.

CHRISTIE, EMMA STRATTON

50. Peavy, Linda and Smith, Ursula. WOMEN IN WAITING
IN THE WESTWARD MOVEMENT: PAMELIA DILLIN
FERGUS AND EMMA STRATTON CHRISTIE.
Montana 1985 35(2): 2-17.

The men who came to the Montana frontier frequently left their
wives and families awaiting their return. With their husbands
absent, these "women in waiting" assumed new responsibilities
managing farms and businesses as well as households. The lives
of these "widows" form a heretofore unexamined element of the
frontier experience. The letters between Pamelia Dillin Fergus
(1824-87) and James Fergus (1813-1902), and Emma Stratton
Christie (1854-1921) and David Christie (1848-1920) portray
the growth of self-reliance and independence among the
"widows" as they endured their husbands' absences. These traits
served them well when they rejoined their husbands on the
frontier.

CLARK, WILLIAM

51. Holt, Glen E. AFTER THE JOURNEY WAS OVER: THE ST. LOUIS YEARS OF LEWIS AND CLARK. *Gateway Heritage 1981 2(2): 42-48.*

Returning to St. Louis on 23 September 1806, explorers Meriwether Lewis and William Clark had completed their historic journey to the Pacific coast. Afterwards Lewis saw his repute sullied and suffered financial reverses before he died in 1809, either a victim of murder or suicide. Clark resided at St. Louis until his death in 1833, becoming one of the city's most prominent citizens. He held important federal posts including an Indian affairs superintendency and the office of surveyor general for Illinois, Missouri, and Arkansas.

CLARKSON BROTHERS

52. Staab, Rodney, ed. THE MATTHEW CLARKSON MANUSCRIPTS. *Kansas Hist. 1982 5(4): 256-278.*

Matthew Flint Clarkson arrived at Hays City, Kansas, in 1868. He was joined by his brothers Charles Ross and George Bernard. They soon became buffalo hunters, during their career killing some 22,000 of the beasts. They were only three of many thousands of men who engaged in this bloody business, but Matthew was one of the few to leave a written record reflecting the viewpoint of actual participants. Most buffalo hunters passed from the scene quickly, but the Clarksons remained in Kansas. Matthew's records provide a sustained perspective on the successive occupations of teamster, woodcutter, hunter, rancher, and farmer.

CONNER, WILLIAM

53. Larson, John L. and Vanderstel, David G. AGENT OF EMPIRE: WILLIAM CONNER ON THE INDIANA FRONTIER, 18OO-1855. *Indiana Mag. of Hist. 1984 80(4): 301-328.*

William Conner lived two separate lives on the Indiana frontier. As Indian trader and agent he organized the exchange of commodities between Indians and fur-trading companies; he also helped in relocating the Delaware tribe from Indiana to Missouri. As a pioneer white settler he became a land speculator, town founder, and merchant banker who traded farm crops for supplies. His early presence in Indiana and his immersion in Delaware Indian culture made it possible for him simultaneously to represent Indians and white settlers.

COOLEY, CORYDON ELIPHALET

54. Welsh, Michael E. CORYDON E. COOLEY: PIONEER IN TWO WORLDS.
J. of Arizona Hist. 1979 20(3): 283-296.

An account of the career of Corydon Eliphalet Cooley (1836-1917) New Mexico and Arizona trader, scout, soldier, miner, rancher, US Marshall and local politician. Having married the two daughters of a White Mountain Apache chief, and operating the largest ranch in the area he was a major influence in bridging the gap between the two cultures, promoting understanding, and stimulating settlement.

COOPER, FANNIE ADAMS

55. Whitlow, Leonard A. and Whitlow, Catherine Cooper, ed. MY LIFE AS A HOMESTEADER (PART 1).
Oregon Hist. Q. 1981 82(1): 65-84.

Memoirs by Fannie Adams Cooper on the experiences and hardships of homesteading in various wild sections of Oregon in the 1890's. There were boundary problems, wild animals, lack of money and frequent moves for her growing family.

56. Whitlow, Leonard A. and Whitlow, Catherine Cooper, ed. MY LIFE AS A HOMESTEADER (PART 2).
Oregon Hist. Q. 1981 82(2): 152-168.

Continued from a previous article. Reminiscences of Fannie Adams Cooper (d. 1942) describe her occupations and relocations and those of her family members in various parts of Oregon from 1899 through the mid-1930's.

COSLEY, JOSEPH CLARENCE

57. DeSanto, Jerome S. THE LEGENDARY JOE COSLEY. *Montana 1980 30(1): 12-27.*

Joseph Clarence Cosley (1870-1944) trapped in the Glacier National Park region and in northern Alberta and Saskatchewan from the mid-1890's until his death in 1944. An admirer of John G. (Kootenai) Brown, Cosley also wrote prose and poetry and became well known for his exotic dress, flowery speech, and fanciful story telling: creating his own legend which survives in Glacier Park today. During 1910-14, Cosley was one of the Park's first rangers. He left to join the Canadian Army during World War I, then returned to trapping (illegally) in the Park until 1929, and then in Canada. In the Belly River region of the Park, Cosley Lake and Cosley Ridge bear his name and several trees survive with his name carved on them.

CROWFOOT, JOE

58. Gooderham, George H. JOE CROWFOOT. *Alberta Hist. (Canada) 1984 32(4): 26-28.*

Profiles the life of Blackfoot Indian Joe Crowfoot. He married Maggie Spotted Eagle in 1921 and became a successful farmer in Alberta. In the 1930's he was made a tribal councillor. He fought for reform of restrictions on Indians and in 1953 was elected a tribal chief.

CUNNINGHAM, CHARLES OLIVER

59. Hassler, David W. CHARLES O. CUNNINGHAM: CALIFORNIA-ARIZONA PIONEER, 1852-1865. *Arizona and the West 1985 27(3): 253-268.*

During the 1850's, Charles Oliver Cunningham crossed the continent and settled in California, to the east of Los Angeles. He established a family, soon became active in local Democratic politics, held minor judicial posts, and opened a general store on his small farm. In 1862, he began carrying freight to the new gold mines in the southwestern Arizona Colorado River country. Soon he became involved in mining silver, lead, copper, and · gold, generally on a speculative basis in the new Arizona

Territory. He died a victim of Indian resistance to continued miner incursions on their homeland. Cunningham was a typical small-time frontier speculator-capitalist.

CUSTER, GEORGE A.

60. Hofling, Charles K. CUSTER'S MARRIAGE AND DOMESTIC LIFE.
Psychohistory Rev. 1980 9(1): 59-70.

General George A. Custer's marriage to Elizabeth Bacon in 1864 was a strong influence on his career. Husband and wife were very close and their memoirs and correspondence reveal considerable dependence on one another. Elizabeth "Libbie" Custer often accompanied her husband, and he encouraged her presence. Briefly examines whether Custer was sterile.

61. Millbrook, Minnie Dubbs. BIG GAME HUNTING WITH THE CUSTERS, 1869-1870.
Kansas Hist. Q. 1975 41(4): 429-453.

General Custer concluded his book, *My Life on the Plains,* with a comment that he had excluded reference to his hunting adventures, although these experiences were in many respects among the most interesting of his recollections. He related some of his experiences at a later date in sporting magazines, but this is the first attempt to describe his hunting experiences while stationed at Fort Hays on the basis of contemporary documents. In addition to regular shooting expeditions in which most officers participated, Custer took part in several hunts during these two years which were specially arranged for tourists from Europe and the East.

D

DAVIS, PERRY EUGENE

62. Gossard, Wayne H., Jr., ed. LIFE ON THE TRAIL: THE 1894 DIARY OF PERRY EUGENE DAVIS.
Colorado Heritage 1981 (1): 23-35.

Real cowboy life did not correspond with that of legend. The 1894 diary of Perry Eugene Davis describing his experiences on a horse-drive from South Dakota to Texas helps set the record straight, expressing the monotony, hard work, and the dangers of the drive. It also reveals the difficulties of finding food and water and crossing areas where fences had been built.

DAY, SAM (FAMILY)

63.   Trafzer, Clifford E.   SAM DAY AND HIS BOYS: GOOD NEIGHBORS TO THE NAVAJOS.
J. of Arizona Hist. 1977 18(1): 1-22.

Sam Day (1845-1925) and his family moved to Arizona in 1883 where he was commissioned to survey an extension of the Navajo reservation. In initial contacts he established mutual respect with the Navajo Indians who almost universally distrusted whites. Later, the Days moved to a trading post where they "became part of the Navajo life pattern" and devoted their energies helping the Navajo to achieve self-sufficiency. They found markets for Navajo sheep, wool, cattle, blankets, and jewelry. In return they brought in wagons, farm tools, household items, and clothing. A grandson is a tribal official today.

DEANE, SILAS

64.   Anderson, Dennis Kent and Anderson, Godfrey Tryggve. THE DEATH OF SILAS DEANE: ANOTHER OPINION.
New England Quarterly 1984 57(1): 98-105.

Silas Deane was a representative to the Continental Congress from Connecticut, worked as a confidential agent in France in 1776, and enlisted the aid of military men such as Lafayette, Steuben, and Pulaski in the American Revolution. Deane was later accused of corruption by the Continental Congress and began to write disparaging letters about the revolution, urging reconciliation with England. On 23 September 1789, after living six years in England, Deane died on board an American ship while waiting for it to leave port and sail for America. Deane's physician, Dr. Edward Bancroft, supported the idea that Deane had taken his own life, and this view was widely accepted for the next few years. Nonetheless, some have maintained that Dr. Bancroft, an expert in the natural history and poisons of Guiana, did him in. A more careful review of Deane's letters, however, indicates that he suffered from a chronic pulmonary condition, probably tuberculosis, and a compelling case can be made that this chronic condition helped bring about a cerebral hemorrhage that caused his death.

DEL VALLE FAMILY

65. Griswold del Castillo, Richard. THE DEL VALLE FAMILY AND THE FANTASY HERITAGE. *California Hist. 1980 59(1): 2-15.*

Traces the fortunes of the del Valle family from the founding of Rancho San Francisco in 1839 to the death of Reginaldo del Valle in 1938. As upper-class Mexican Californians, the del Valle family survived and prospered through good luck and efficient management as California's population increasingly was dominated by Anglo-Americans after statehood. From 1841 to 1924, in the Santa Clara valley near today's Oxnard and Ventura, the family successfully operated its Rancho Camulos, one of the locales said to be the inspiration for Helen Hunt Jackson's *Ramona*. The family's partial acceptance of the pseudo-Spanish fantasy heritage had some virtues as Mexicanos and new Anglo-American immigrants found that heritage an easy one to adopt.

DEMOSS, NETTIE

66. DeMoss, Nettie; Crone, Norman, ed. INDIAN TERRITORY MEMORIES. *Chronicles of Oklahoma 1981 59(1): 106-110.*

Recounts the author's reminiscences of homesteading near Peggs, Oklahoma from 1896 to 1915 and the fear of Indians. The family moved to Tahlequah in 1915 and soon thereafter to Sand Springs where the oil boom was underway. The author married and took a job with the City Welfare Department during the economic hard times of the 1920's and 1930's.

DENSMORE, FRANCES

67. Archabal, Nina Marchetti. FRANCES DENSMORE:
PIONEER IN THE STUDY OF AMERICAN INDIAN MUSIC.
Stuhler, Barbara and Kreuter, Gretchen, ed.
*Women of Minnesota: Selected Biographical Essays (St. Paul:
Minnesota Historical Society Press, 1977): 94-115.*

Frances Densmore (1867-1957) was born and raised in Red
Wing, Minnesota, where the sight of Indians was common.
Densmore was formally trained in 18th- and 19th-century
European music; her scholarly research in Native American
music made her a pioneer in ethnomusicology. Alice
Cunningham Fletcher and John Comfort Fillmore especially
influenced Densmore when she began her studies of Indian
music in the 1890's. From then until her death in 1957,
Densmore studied, recorded, analyzed, and published
monographs on the music of the Chippewa, Teton Sioux,
Papago, Arapaho, Ute, Mandan, Zuni, and many other Indians.
The Bureau of American Ethnology financially supported her
work, and she collected more than 2,400 wax cylinders of
Native American music. Densmore gradually evolved a theory
and understanding of Indian music which appreciated its cultural
context and recognized it as "profoundly different" from
Western musical tradition.

DESHA, MARY

68. Klotter, James C. and Klotter, Freda Campbell. MARY
DESHA, ALASKAN SCHOOLTEACHER OF 1888.
Pacific Northwest Q. 1980 71(2): 78-86.

Presents excerpts from the letters of Mary Desha (1850-1911),
who in 1888, set out from her comfortable parents' home in
Lexington, Kentucky, for the frontier settlement of Sitka,
Alaska, where she had accepted a teaching position. Many of
her letters praised the natural beauty of Alaska, but she
simultaneously held a strong contempt for most of the Indian,
Russian, and Yankee population encountered there. In some
ways Mary Desha proved flexible in adapting to frontier
conditions, but she could not escape the biases endemic to a
true, unreconstructed southerner. Following her return from
Alaska, she became heavily involved with the Daughters of the

American Revolution and the United Daughters of the Confederacy.

DIMOND, ANTHONY J.

69. Mangusso, Mary Childers. TONY DIMOND FINDS HIS FUTURE, AFTER CAREER AS MINER FAILS TO PAN OUT.
Alaska Journal 1982 12(4): 12-23.

Anthony Dimond went to Alaska in 1905 to find gold and adventure, but his prospecting career was cut short when he accidentally shot himself in the leg. He studied law, was admitted to the bar, and eventually embarked on a political career and became the territory's single, nonvoting delegate to Congress.

DRAGGING CANOE

70. Evans, E. Raymond. NOTABLE PERSONS IN CHEROKEE HISTORY: DRAGGING CANOE.
J. of Cherokee Studies 1977 2(1): 176-189.

Dragging Canoe was born about 1740 in an Overhill town on the Little Tennessee River and became a military leader in maturity. He opposed any land cessions to the whites, sided with the British during the American Revolution, and personally led many attacks. Following the Revolution he was involved in attempts to form an Indian alliance against the Americans. The defeat of St. Clair in November 1791 was a highlight of his career. He died 1 March 1792 at Lookout Mountain, Tennessee.

DREW, JOHN THOMPSON

71. McFadden, Marguerite. COLONEL JOHN THOMPSON DREW: CHEROKEE CAVALIER.
Chronicles of Oklahoma 1981 59(1): 30-53.

John Thompson Drew, mixed-blood Cherokee, played a key role in tribal history because of his ability to speak English, his businessman's acumen, and his powerful relatives. Despite a lack of formal education, Drew was licensed to practice law in

1851 and within two years was made Judge of the Canadian District of Indian Territory. During the Civil War he actively supported the Confederacy by raising a regiment of Cherokee soldiers, but the war destroyed his wealth.

DULUTH, DANIEL GREYSOLON, SIEUR

72. Dunn, James Taylor. DU LUTH'S BIRTHPLACE: A FOOTNOTE TO HISTORY.
Minnesota Hist. 1979 46(6): 228-232.

Many historians have incorrectly indicated that the birthplace of Daniel Greysolon, Sieur Du Luth, was Saint-Germain-en-Laye, a suburb of Paris. In the early 1950's, a Canadian historian, Gerald Malchelosse, and a French local historian, Doctor Attale Boel, correctly identified Saint-Germain-Laval in the Forez region as the birthplace of this 17th-century French explorer of the New World. The lack of extant records makes an exact date of birth impossible to ascertain, but evidence strongly suggests that Greysolon was born in that town between 1636 and 1640. His family was of the petty nobility.

E

EDE, SUSANNA

73. Zimmerman, Barbara Baker and Carstensen, Vernon. PIONEER WOMAN IN SOUTHWESTERN WASHINGTON TERRITORY: THE RECOLLECTIONS OF SUSANNA MARIA SLOVER MC FARLAND PRICE EDE.
Pacific Northwest Q. 1976 67(4): 137-150.

Reminiscences of Susanna Ede (1854-1937), whose pioneer life was spent along the lower Chehalis River, Grays Harbor, and the Copalis Beach area of Washington Territory. Widowed by William McFarland at age 26, she twice remarried, first to Dr. J. B. Price, physician at the Quinault Indian Agency, and later to Walter Ede whom she later divorced. Susanna described her log cabin life during the 1870's, her position as teacher and government interpreter at the Quinault Agency, bouts with timber wolves, and the production of home remedies and canned foods.

ELSNER, JOHN

74. Hornbein, Marjorie. DR. JOHN ELSNER, A COLORADO PIONEER. *Western States Jewish Hist. Q. 1981 13(4): 291-302.*

Dr. John Elsner (1844-1922) came to Denver, Colorado, in 1866 on a mining venture. He settled into medical practice and became a leader in the organization of city and state medical societies in 1871. With his wife, Lena, he was active in the Jewish community, helping to establish the B'nai B'rith Lodge and Congregation Emmanuel. In 1889 he participated in the founding of the National Jewish Hospital.

ELY, EDMUND F.

75. Hoover, Roy. "TO STAND ALONE IN THE WILDERNESS": EDMUND F. ELY, MISSIONARY. *Minnesota History 1985 49(7): 265-280.*

Presents the life and observations of Edmund F. Ely (1809-1882), who served as a lay missionary and teacher for the American Board of Commissioners for Foreign Missions among the Chippewa Indians in northern Minnesota and Wisconsin during 1833-49. His journals report much about his journey there and the first encounters with the land, the Indians, the work, and his competition and co-workers. While the years gave him more relaxed expectations about them all, he also acquired a large family and left his lonely occupation on the frontier.

ETCHART, CATHERINE URQUILUX

76. Urza, Monique. CATHERINE ETCHART: A MONTANA LOVE STORY. *Montana 1981 31(1): 2-17.*

John Etchart and his wife, Catherine Urquilux Etchart, operated a sheep ranch near Glasgow, in Valley County, Montana. Both were French Basques. He came to the United States in 1900 and worked with sheep in California and Nevada before settling in Montana in 1910. Catherine came as a bride in 1912. They dealt with problems of winter weather, homesteaders, and isolation; they employed other Basques to help herd sheep. After John's death in 1943, Catherine managed the ranch operation until her own death in 1978. She was active and frugal, and donated to various Catholic charities.

EVANS, JOHN

77. Williams, Gwyn A. JOHN EVANS'S MISSION TO THE MADOGWYS 1792-1799.
Bull. of the Board of Celtic Studies (Great Britain) 1978 27(4): 569-601.

Describes the epic journey in quest of Welsh Indians by John Evans (1770-99), explorer and pioneer colonialist. Evans left his birthplace, Waun-fawr, Caernarvonshire, probably in 1792 and traveled to Baltimore in search of adventure. After many reverses, he succeeded in making a map of the Missouri, traded with the Indians, and became a surveyor in upper Louisiana; but frustrations to his empire-building projects led him to the heavy drinking from which he died.

F

FINK, MIKE.

78. Allen, Michael. "SIRED BY A HURRICANE": MIKE FINK, WESTERN BOATMEN AND THE MYTH OF THE ALLIGATOR HORSE.
Arizona and the West 1985 27(3): 237-252.

Western Pennsylvania frontiersman Mike Fink worked as a keelboatman on the Ohio and Mississippi rivers. He soon gained a reputation as a good boatman, a hard drinker, and a volatile fighter. Constantly at odds with the law and uncomfortable with advancing civilization, he kept moving west. He died on the Upper Missouri fur trapping frontier. Fink's reputation grew to mythic proportions, to the extent that he became known as the king of the "half horse, half alligator" Western boatmen.

79. Ross, Jane. FEISTY FINK, KING OF BATTLING BOATMEN ON "THE BIG RIVER." *Smithsonian 1979 10(1): 98-102.*

Discusses the life and legend of Mike Fink, the archetypal keelboatman, 1770-1823.

FITZPATRICK, RICHARD

80. Black, Hugo L., III. RICHARD FITZPATRICK'S SOUTH FLORIDA, 1822-1840. *Tequesta 1980 40: 47-77; 1981 41: 33-68.*

Part I. KEY WEST PHASE. Richard Fitzpatrick left his native Columbia, South Carolina, around 1816. He moved to Key West in 1822; where his activities included involvement in the wrecking industry, salt industry, election to the 1831 and 1832 legislative councils, and slavery. Based on chancery records, court papers in the Monroe County Public Library, and microfilm copies of records housed in the P. K. Yonge Library, Gainesville; 97 notes. Part II. FITZPATRICK'S MIAMI RIVER PLANTATION. Fitzpatrick paid John Egan $400.00 for 640 acres on the Miami River in 1830. After continued purchases he had acquired 2,660 acres on the Miami River and 640 acres on the New River. He established a plantation on the Miami River, attempting to establish a planter society in south Florida. Slaves concentrated on the growing of sugar cane. Before the Second Seminole War ruined his efforts, driving him from Florida in 1840, Fitzpatrick had been one of the most powerful and active members of the Legislative Council of Florida. Elected President of the Council in 1836, he had Dade County created in south Florida.

FLOYD, JOHN

81. Hammon, Neal and Harris, James Russell, ed. "IN A DANGEROUS SITUATION": LETTERS OF COL. JOHN FLOYD, 1774-1783. *Register of the Kentucky Historical Society 1985 83(3): 202-236.*

Prints 19 letters of John Floyd, a surveyor who spent much time on the frontiers in Kentucky. His letters, dated 1774-83, tell of his views on events of the time and of the difficulties of life on the frontier. Although Floyd went West to survey, he spent much of his time in conflict with Indians and was killed in an ambush in 1783.

FOOY, BENJAMIN

82. Roper, James E.   BENJAMIN FOOY AND THE SPANISH FORTS OF SAN FERNANDO AND CAMPO DE LA ESPERANZA.
West Tennessee Hist. Soc. Papers 1982 36: 41-64.

An immigrant from Holland, Benjamin Fooy first appears in American history in 1782, when he was living among the Chickasaw Indians. Versed in both the Chickasaw and Choctaw tongues, Fooy served as an interpreter and diplomat for Spain among the Indians. He was witness to the numerous political changes in the Memphis area after the Revolutionary War, when the Spaniards abandoned Fort San Fernando in what is now Memphis and built Fort Campo de la Esperanza just across the Mississippi River in Arkansas. The latter fort passed into French hands and then was acquired by the United States as part of the Louisiana Purchase in 1803. Fooy weathered the political changes well, serving as diplomat, trader, and judge. He ended his days as a valued citizen and official.

FORD, AUGUSTUS

83. Palmer, Richard F.   LAKE ONTARIO'S FIRST CHARTMAKER.
Inland Seas 1983 39(2): 91-95.

Captain Augustus Ford moved to Oswego, New York, in 1797. He served on board lake ships before joining the navy in 1810 as a master on the *Oneida*. In 1813 he drew three charts of Lake Ontario, which Commodore Isaac Chauncey promised, but failed, to have published. Ford served at the Sackets Harbor Naval Station for 20 years and died in 1855.

FOREMAN, STEPHEN

84. Evans, E. Raymond. NOTABLE PERSONS IN CHEROKEE HISTORY: STEPHEN FOREMAN. *J. of Cherokee Studies 1977 2(2): 230-239.*

Stephen Foreman was born on 22 October 1807 in north Georgia, the son of Anthony Foreman, a Scottish soldier, and Elizabeth Foreman. He was educated for the ministry at Candy's Creek and New Echota, Georgia, and at Union and Princeton Theological Seminaries. In 1833 he was licensed to preach by the Presbyterian Church. He led one group of Cherokee Indians west during the removal of the 1830's. After settling in Park Hill, Oklahoma, he was active in Cherokee government and established a school system. During this time he also translated parts of the Bible from Greek to Cherokee. He died in Oklahoma on 8 December 1881.

FREE, MICKEY (FELIX WARD)

85. Radbourne, Allan. THE NAMING OF MICKEY FREE. *J. of Arizona Hist. 1976 17(3): 341-346.*

Twelve-year-old Felix Ward was abducted by the White Mountain Apache in an 1861 raid on an Arizona ranch. He later attained renown as Mickey Free, interpreter and Apache Scout. Gives a more probable explanation of how Felix Ward came to be called Mickey Free than ones conjectured by previous writers.

FRENCH, LEIGH HILL

86. French, Leigh Hill. NOME NUGGETS. *Alaska J. 1983 13(4): 33-63.*

Presents a personal account of life in Nome, Alaska, during the 1900 gold rush by Leigh Hill French, one of the participants. Seeking his fortune, French shipped a mining machine to Nome to dig gold from the seabed off the coast of Nome. This venture ended in disaster. Despite some inaccuracies and plagiarism, French's is one of the best accounts of the Alaskan gold rush.

G

GALT, JAMES AND WILLIAM, JR.

87. Herndon, G. Melvin. FROM SCOTTISH ORPHAN TO
VIRGINIA PLANTER: WILLIAM GALT, JR. 1801-1851.
Virginia Mag. of Hist. and Biog. 1979 87(3): 326-343.

Galt, an orphan, was educated in England and brought to
America by a wealthy Virginia relative of the same name. From
1817 Galt, Jr., helped his foster father in business, and inherited
some of his extensive lands in 1825, which he farmed with
sound technique until his death. Galt educated his children, was
paternalistic toward his slaves, was a philanthropist, a strong
Whig but no office-seeker, and a regular if somewhat eccentric
churchgoer.

88. Herndon, G. Melvin. FROM ORPHANS TO
MERCHANTS TO PLANTERS: THE GALT BROTHERS,
WILLIAM AND JAMES.
Virginia Cavalcade 1979 29(1): 22-31.

William (1800-51) and James (1805-76) Galt, brothers orphaned
in Scotland, arrived in Virginia in the early 19th century and
became wealthy and well-known planters and humane
slaveholders, and actively supported the Confederacy.

GERONIMO

89. Brown, Dee. GERONIMO.
Am. Hist. Illus. 1980 15(3): 12-21, (4): 36-45.

Part I. Discusses the activities and reputation of Geronimo,
leader of the Chiricahua Apache, who became a legend created
by the press in the 1870's, 20 years after he became a legend
among his own people. Part II. Continues the story of
Geronimo's exploits from 1881, when he led the Chiricahua to
Mexico from the Sierra Madre, until 1909, when he succumbed
to pneumonia.

GIRTY, SIMON

90. Richards, James K. A CLASH OF CULTURES: SIMON GIRTY AND THE STRUGGLE FOR THE FRONTIER. *Timeline 1985 2(3): 2-17.*

Discusses the life of Pennsylvania-born Simon Girty, his 1778 defection to the British side and participation in the Revolutionary War fighting with Indian enemies of colonials on the northern frontier, and speculates on the accuracy of reports of Girty's cruelty and barbarity.

GRAPPE, FRANCOIS

91. Grappe, Bernie. FRANCOIS GRAPPE: UNIQUE NORTH LOUISIANA FRONTIERSMAN. *North Louisiana Hist. Assoc. J. 1978 9(2): 65-70.*

Discusses the character, life, and career of Francois Grappe (1747-1825), whose contribution to North Louisiana history has been neglected. He served as Indian agent and interpreter for France, Spain, and the United States. His name is associated with the controversial "Grappe Reservation" of the Caddo Indian Treaty of 1835, but wrongly, because he had died a decade earlier. Colorful and gifted with an impressive knowledge of North Louisiana geography and Indian languages, he was held in high esteem.

GRAYSON, WILLIAM

92. Horrell, Joseph, ed. NEW LIGHT ON WILLIAM GRAYSON: HIS GUARDIAN'S ACCOUNT. *Virginia Mag. of Hist. and Biog. 1984 92(4): 423-443.*

Biographers have paid little attention to the youth of Founding Father William Grayson, a Revolutionary War colonel and senator from Virginia. Grayson was orphaned at 16, and his elder brother Benjamin was appointed guardian of William's estate. Benjamin's account books provide a good record of William's education, travel, and expenses from age 16 to 20. They also reveal that Benjamin was a highly irresponsible businessman. These accounts are unusual because they reveal the rarely seen documentation of an 18th-century youth's lifestyle.

GRINNELL, JOSEPH

93. Grinnell, Elizabeth, ed. GOLD HUNTING IN ALASKA AS TOLD BY JOSEPH GRINNELL. *Alaska J. 1983 13(2): 33-111.*

Reprints diaries of Joseph Grinnell, who prospected for gold in the Kotzebue Sound region of Alaska. The diaries, edited by his mother and first published around 1901, contain many details about daily life and personal narratives about the gold rush.

H

HALDIMAND, FREDERICK

94. Rea, Robert R. BRIGADIER FREDERICK HALDIMAND—THE FLORIDA YEARS. *Florida Hist. Q. 1976 54(4): 512-531.*

Brigadier Frederick Haldimand (1718-1791), assigned responsibility for the Floridas by General Thomas Gage, arrived in Pensacola in 1767. Haldimand immediately rebuilt the dilapidated fort, ordered gardens planted, land drained, and a hospital constructed. After Anglo-Spanish tensions of the early 1770's relaxed, Haldimand's tenure at Pensacola was quiet. In 1773 Haldimand left Florida to become Gage's temporary successor as commander-in-chief of North America while Gage was on leave.

HANSON, JOHN

95. Carlsson, Sten and Nordstrom, Byron J., transl. JOHN HANSON'S SWEDISH BACKGROUND. *Swedish Pioneer Hist. Q. 1978 29(1): 9-20.*

A genealogical study based on work in 1876 by George A. Hanson, a Maryland lawyer. John Hanson was one of

Maryland's two great forefathers and a political activist during the American Revolution. He was President of Congress in Philadelphia in 1781-82. He was born in either 1715 or 1721 and died in 1783. In 1903 a statue was erected over his grave in Statuary Hall in the Capitol in Washington, D.C. Concludes that George Hanson established a clear set of traditions which do include genealogical links with Sweden.

HARDIN, JOHN WESLEY

96. McGinty, Brian. JOHN WESLEY HARDIN: GENTLEMAN OF GUNS.
Am. Hist. Illus. 1982 17(4): 32-36.

John Wesley Hardin, who considered himself a "gentleman of guns" rather than a "gunman" of the Old West, killed over 20 men before he was 25 and was sent to the Texas State Penitentiary at Huntsville.

HELLIER, THOMAS

97. Breen, T. H.; Lewis, James H.; and Schlesinger, Keith. MOTIVE FOR MURDER: A SERVANT'S LIFE IN VIRGINIA, 1678.
William and Mary Q. 1983 40(1): 106-120.

On 24 May 1678 Thomas Hellier, a 28-year-old indentured servant, murdered with an axe Cuthbert Williamson, Williamson's wife, and a young servant girl at a Charles City County plantation, known as Hard Labour. Immediately captured, he confessed. The night before his execution Hellier told his life story to an Anglican minister, presumed to have been Paul Williams. The narrative of Hellier's life, the minister's comments, and the condemned man's final speech at the gallows were published as *The Vain Prodigal Life* (1680), and sections of the pamphlet are reprinted here. Surprisingly the minister's reflections are sociological, and the Williamsons were much to be blamed themselves for the tragedy because of their abusive treatment of servants.

HICKOK, JAMES BUTLER "WILD BILL"

98. Rosa, Joseph G. J. B. HICKOK, DEPUTY U.S. MARSHAL.
Kansas Hist. 1979 2(4): 231-251.

James Butler "Wild Bill" Hickok (1837-76) was a scout, teamster, wagonmaster, and frontier lawman in Kansas from 1856 to 1871. A semifictional article about "Wild Bill" in the February 1867 issue of *Harper's New Monthly Magazine* launched the move to romanticize him as a great pistoleer. As a deputy US marshal from 1867 to 1871, Hickok was caught up in the less exciting duties of arresting counterfeiters, deserters from the army, those who stole government property, and those who murdered Indians on and off the reservation. Much time was spent testifying at trials and aiding state officials pursuing murderers.

HOLLADAY, JOHN

99. Holladay, Alvis M.; Holladay, Robert B.; and Holladay, Wendell G. SPENCER'S COMPANION: WHO WAS HE?
Tennessee Hist. Q. 1980 39(3): 282-291.

Traces the history of John Holladay (ca. 1745-1812) who accompanied Thomas Sharpe Spencer and several other first white settlers to middle Tennessee in 1776. Holladay came west from Bedford County, Virginia. He did not "desert" his friend Spencer in 1777 as legend has it, but he did eventually return to Virginia and his family.

HOOVER, JACOB "JAKE"

100. Jensen, Earl L. RUSSELL'S FIRST FRIEND IN MONTANA.
Montana 1984 34(3): 24-33.

In 1881 Charles M. Russell, the cowboy artist, met Jacob "Jake" Hoover along the Judith River in central Montana. Hoover, an experienced trapper and prospector, invited the tenderfoot Russell to live with him, and they became close friends. During the 1880's, Russell spent a great deal of time at Hoover's cabin, first as a cabin mate, later as a regular guest. From Hoover, who had come to Montana from Iowa at the age of 16, Russell learned the skills needed to survive on the Montana frontier. Hoover, who appeared in several Russell paintings, joined the gold rush to Alaska in the late 1890's, then returned to Seattle in 1908, where he remained until his death in 1925.

HOUSTON, SAM

101. Corn, James F. SAM HOUSTON: THE RAVEN.
J. of Cherokee Studies 1981 6(1): 34-49.

Sam Houston's early life among Western Cherokees of North Carolina included their adoption of him. Named Ku-lanu (the Raven) by Oo-loo-to-ka (John Jolly), Houston led the Cherokees against the Creeks in the Battle of Horseshoe Bend (27 May 1814), served as Cherokee representative in Washington, D.C., and mediated border disputes for the Cherokees with Pawnees and Osages. Later, Houston traveled to Texas, led settlers for independence, and became Texas's first president.

102. Frantz, Joe B. TEXAS GIANT OF CONTRADICTIONS: SAM HOUSTON.
Am. West 1980 17(4): 4-13, 61-65.

Sam (Samuel) Houston (1793-1863) lived a robust and colorful life on the stages of Tennessee, national, and Texas politics, the military, and the Cherokee Indians. His life is a study of extremes and contradictions: a "two-fisted drinker," he became a temperance lecturer; an Indian fighter, at various times he lived with the Cherokee; a Mexican hater, he was magnanimous to his captured enemy commander, General Santa Anna; a devoted husband, he became a bigamist.

J

JEFFORDS, TOM

103. Cramer, Harry G., III. TOM JEFFORDS—INDIAN AGENT.
J. of Arizona Hist. 1976 17(3): 265-300.

When Cochise, the Chiricahua Apache chief, surrendered in 1872 and agreed that his people would live on a newly created reservation in southeastern Arizona, his one stipulation was that Tom Jeffords (1832-1914) must be the agent. Captain Thomas Jefferson Jeffords, the confidant of Cochise, had been instrumental in the surrender. Narrates the efforts of Jeffords to make the treaty work despite the counterefforts of the government to reduce the Apache to complete dependence. With a series of incidents and the termination of the reservation in 1876, the peace broke down and the Chiricahua reverted to their prior state of warfare.

K

KITCHEN, PETER

104. Snoke, Elizabeth R. PETE KITCHEN: ARIZONA PIONEER.
Arizona and the West 1979 21(3): 235-256.

Peter Kitchen (1819-95) was the epitome of a successful pioneer who gave stability to the southwest frontier. He arrived in Arizona in 1854 and established himself in cattle and farming. He developed a profitable business supplying meat, grain, and vegetables to southern Arizona communities, mines, and military posts. He bought and sold interests in local mines. Kitchen moved to Tucson in 1883 to spend the rest of his life in real estate, gambling, and civic events. He has become a legendary frontier folk hero.

KWAH, CHIEF

105. Bishop, Charles A. KWAH: A CARRIER CHIEF.
Judd, Carol M. and Ray, Arthur J., ed.
Old Trails and New Directions: Papers of the Third North American Fur Trade Conference (Toronto: U. of Toronto Pr., 1980): 191-204.

Presents a biography of Kwah (1755-1840), chief of the Stuart Lake Carrier Indians. He provided fish for the Fort St. James trading post next to his village and the headquarters of the New

Caledonia fur emporium, spared the life of a future governor, and became the most important chief among the Carrier associated with Fort St. James. Although he undoubtedly had inherited his title, and although he also had the good fortune to have been the chief of the village adjacent to the trading post, he possessed all of the necessary qualities of a leader. In addition to a prominent place in the history of the Hudson's Bay Company's New Caledonia fur trade, he left a progeny of 16 children so that today over half of the Stuart Lake Indians claim descent.

L

LASSEN, PETER

106. Scott, Franklin D. PETER LASSEN: DANISH PIONEER OF CALIFORNIA, 1800-1859.
Lovoll, Odd S., ed.
Makers of an American Immigrant Legacy: Essays in Honor of Kenneth O. Bjork (Northfield, Minn.: Norwegian-American Hist. Assoc., 1980): 186-209.

Danish blacksmith, Peter Lassen (1800-59) immigrated to Boston in 1830; he moved to California in 1839, living as a true frontiersman until killed by Indians in 1859.

107. Scott, Franklin D. PETER LASSEN: DANISH PIONEER OF CALIFORNIA.
Southern California Q. 1981 63(2): 113-136.

A profile of Peter Lassen (1800-59), pioneer settler in northern California. Born in Denmark, Lassen became a blacksmith but found conditions in his homeland unsettled. He came to America in 1830, met John Sutter, and in 1840 arrived in California. He established California's northernmost rancho in the Mexican period and operated the first sawmill in the area. Following the Mexican War he led a wagon train to northern California along what became known as the Lassen Trail. Mount Lassen is named for him, as is Lassen Pass, and other landmarks. Travelers remembered his hospitality, but his desire to help people conflicted with his ambitions for economic success. In the 1850's he operated a ranch in the isolated northeastern corner of the state. He was killed by Indians in 1859 under mysterious circumstances.

LAWE, JOHN

108. Kay, Jeanne. JOHN LAWE, GREEN BAY TRADER. *Wisconsin Mag. of Hist. 1980 64(1): 2-27.*

John Lawe, a Jewish fur trader who operated out of Green Bay and who attained the status of bourgeois, never achieved the success of many of his associates such as Ramsay Crooks and Robert Stuart of the American Fur Company. Lawe's experience, first as a clerk for Jacob Franks, then as a trader for the American Fur Company, and finally as a land owner and speculator, never led to great wealth on the Wisconsin frontier.

LEWIS, MERIWETHER

109. Abrams, Rochanne. MERIWETHER LEWIS: THE LOGISTICAL IMAGINATION. *Missouri Hist. Soc. Bull. 1980 36(4): 228-240.*

President Thomas Jefferson placed Meriwether Lewis and William Clark in charge of an expedition to explore the American West, 1804-06. The expedition succeeded largely because Lewis spent more than a year, 1803-04, gathering preliminary information, painstakingly planning the journey, assembling equipment and provisions, and anticipating the expedition's needs.

110. Abrams, Rochanne. THE COLONIAL CHILDHOOD OF MERIWETHER LEWIS. *Missouri Hist. Soc. Bull. 1978 34(4): 218-227.*

Remembered primarly for historic western explorations in 1804-06, Meriwether Lewis (1774-1809) spent his early childhood in Albemarle County, Virginia, where he absorbed the code of Virginia gentlemen. Then Lewis experienced frontier harshness when the family moved to Georgia. Later he returned to Virginia for formal education which emphasized the classics but also provided him with a smattering of arithmetic, geography, and natural science.

LINN, WILLIAM

111.   Anderson, Philip J.   WILLIAM LINN, 1752-1808:
AMERICAN REVOLUTIONARY AND ANTI-
JEFFERSONIAN.
J. of Presbyterian Hist. 1977 55(4): 381-394.

The American Calvinist William Linn (1752-1808) was a
typical American Revolutionary clergyman in identifying with
the British all that was evil, with the Americans all that was
righteous. Recognized as an excellent preacher as well as
academician, after the Revolutionary War he held numerous
influential pulpits and was associated with several schools. He
wrote many books, including a life of George Washington. At
first he hailed the French Revolution as an event that would
extend God's activity in bringing liberty to the world, but the
emerging irreligion turned him from it. Thomas Jefferson he
accused of totally removing religion from politics, a course that
could only lead to atheism. He thus stands as a poignant
reminder of the perplexing dilemma which confronted so many
of his clerical generation: the separation of church and state, and
yet the perceived responsibility of the Church to keep
government "Christian."

LITTLE TURTLE (MISHIKINSKWA)

112.   Carter, Harvey Lewis.   A FRONTIER TRAGEDY:
LITTLE TURTLE AND WILLIAM WELLS.
Old Northwest 1980 6(1): 3-18.

Little Turtle (Mishikinskwa) was elected war chief of the Miami
Indians in 1780. The tribe resided on the Eel River in southern
Wisconsin. In 1783 William Wells and three other boys were
captured by an Indian party. Wells was adopted into the family
of the chief, Gaviahatte, and eventually became Little Turtle's
son-in-law by marrying his daughter Sweet Breeze. This article
is the story of Little Turtle and Well's attempt to bridge the gap
between white and Indian culture.

LITTLE WOLF

113.   Roberts, Gary L.   THE SHAME OF LITTLE WOLF.
Montana 1978 28(3): 36-47.

The life of Little Wolf (Northern Cheyenne) reflected the intensely personal dilemma American Indian leaders faced when white domination forced them to abandon their traditional roles and confront the vices of dependence and stagnation. Little Wolf assumed positions of traditional importance as a Cheyenne chief during the 1860's-70's, especially as a Sweet Medicine Chief, who bore the Sacred Bundle. After surrendering to US troops in 1877 and deportation to Indian Territory, Little Wolf, Dull Knife, and 336 followers fled back toward Montana in 1878-79. A portion of the group under Dull Knife surrendered at Ft. Robinson, Kansas. Little Wolf succeeded in leading 114 Cheyenne to Ft. Keogh, Montana. There, Little Wolf developed a strong friendship with Lt. William P. Clark who defended the chief and the cause of the Northern Cheyenne. In 1880, Little Wolf became drunk and killed a rival Cheyenne, Starving Elk. Never before had a Sweet Medicine Chief killed another Cheyenne. He lived until 1904, in seclusion and self-imposed exile along the Rosebud River, as a result of the incident. In 1884, the government created the Tongue River Agency in the area, giving the Northern Cheyenne a permanent home.

LOGAN, ERNEST

114. Schaedel, Grace Logan. THE STORY OF ERNEST AND LIZZIE LOGAN—A FRONTIER COURTSHIP. *Ann. of Wyoming 1982 54(2): 48-61.*

Ernest Logan arrived at Camp Carlin, Wyoming, in 1871 and subsequently worked as a carpenter, cowboy, and stagecoach driver. In 1891 he opened a book and stationery shop in Cheyenne that featured a soda fountain and homemade ice cream and candy. Two years later he married Lizzie Walker who had come west to work with her sister Jennie in a dressmaking business. Together they made the Logan Store one of the lasting business enterprises of Cheyenne.

M

MACKENZIE, ALEXANDER

115. Lavender, David. FIRST CROSSING: ALEXANDER
MACKENZIE'S QUEST FOR THE PACIFIC.
Am. West 1977 14(5): 4-11, 67-68.

Alexander Mackenzie (1763-1820), in the service of the North
West Company, searched for a viable fur-trade route across
Canada to the Pacific. Based on Lake Athabasca, in 1789 he
traveled to Great Slave Lake, discovered the Mackenzie River,
and followed it to the Arctic Ocean. During 1792-93, from the
same base, he followed the Peace River over the Rocky
Mountains, the Parsnip, Fraser, and Bella Coola rivers to the
Pacific. He had made the first crossing of the continent north of
Mexico.

MACOUN, JOHN

116. McGeown, Mary G. JOHN MACOUN.
Alberta Hist. (Canada) 1980 28(2): 16-19.

Emigrating to Canada in 1850 from Ireland, John Macoun
(1831-1920) gained a considerable reputation as a botanist and
explorer in Canada where his name is commemorated by a town
in southern Saskatchewan, a mountain in Glacier National Park,
and a lake in northern Saskatchewan as well as 48 species of
plants which he discovered. Discusses his brief career as a
farmhand in Canada, which was largely self-taught, followed by
10 years as a teacher during which he concentrated on studying
botany and building a herbarium. In 1869, he was offered the
Chair of Natural History in Alberta College, Belleville, Ontario.
In the company of such men as Sandford Fleming and George
Grant while crossing the country, he collected botanical
specimens for his studies. Numerous trips followed, during
which he explored and studied the huge plain of southern
Saskatchewan. His writings include *Manitoba and the Great
North-West* (1882) and his autobiography. He later lived in
Ottawa, then Vancouver.

MARSH, JOHN

117. Stuart, Reginald and Stuart, Winifred. JOHN MARSH.
Pacific Hist. 1980 24(3): 369-375.

Biographical account of John Marsh, the first American to settle on the Contra Costa. In 1828 he was granted a license to practice medicine in the Pueblo of Los Angeles. In 1837 Marsh purchased a large ranchero, Los Meganos. He obtained cattle for his ranch by being paid in cattle for his medical services. He was instrumental in encouraging settlers to come to California to live. The gold discovery in Coloma brought hordes of people to the area and the doctor became a rich man by tending to their needs. After marrying, having a daughter, and then losing his wife to disease, John Marsh became uninterested in life. His long-lost half-Indian son found him and renewed his vitality. A disgruntled worker killed John Marsh and his son chased the murderer and brought him to trial and sentencing. The uncompleted stone mansion still stands on Marsh Road. Covers 1828-55.

MAY, KATE E.

118. Goetz, Henry Kilian. KATE'S QUARTER SECTION: A WOMAN IN THE CHEROKEE STRIP.
Chronicles of Oklahoma 1983 61(3): 246-267.

Kate E. May made the 1893 "rush for land" in the Cherokee Strip, Oklahoma Territory, in an effort to improve the life of her family. Despite the thousands of competitors lined up at the starting point, May outdistanced most of them on her fleet pony and staked a claim on some rich agricultural land south of Perry. She and her children lived out of a covered wagon, defended the land against claim jumpers, and eventually built a frame house. They subsequently opened a small restaurant in Perry to supplement the farm income. In 1895, they left the farm and moved to Oklahoma City because the children needed medical attention.

MAYER, JOE (FAMILY)

119. Thorpe, Winifred L. and Spude, Robert L. JOE MAYER AND HIS TOWN.
J. of Arizona Hist. 1978 19(2): 131-168.

Reminiscences by Joe Mayer's daughter, of the rise and success of Mayer, Arizona, the town founded by her father. From New York, Joe Mayer came to the West via odd jobs, and eventually bought a restaurant and stage station for $3,500 in gold that he developed into a town. Mayer's wife, formerly Sarah Belle Wilbur, came and they built new enterprises. The Mayer family grew: Mary Bell (Mamie), Martha Gertrude (Martie), Wilbur Joseph (Bur), and Winifred (Winnie). Mayer invested in mining; owned the French Lily mine, met outlaws, met Indians, and contested floods. After the flood of 1890, when most of the town was swept away, Mayer rebuilt, with homes, corrals, freight stations, and a schoolhouse. The Santa Fe Railroad built a line to Mayer which then became a center for cattle, sheep, and ore. While investigating a prowler, Joe Mayer accidentally shot himself and died in December 1909. Sarah Mayer suffered a stroke and she died on 11 November 1934.

MCDONALD, ALICE

120. McDonald, Alice. AS WELL AS ANY MAN.
Alaska Journal 1984 14(3): 39-45.

Presents an autobiographical account of the labors of Alice McDonald, a Swedish woman who went to seek her fortune in Alaskan mining camps. She worked as a cook in Dawson for a time, then did odd jobs, such as blueberry picking, baking, and laundering while her husband prospected for gold. She opened a hotel in Iditarod and, when business dwindled, moved to California, where she began writing her memoirs at age 84.

MCKAY, JAMES

121. Goossen, N. Jaye. A WEARER OF MOCCASINS: THE HONOURABLE JAMES MC KAY OF DEER LODGE.
Beaver (Canada) 1978 309(2): 44-53.

James McKay, a Red River Metis, was born at Fort Edmonton in 1828 to an employee of the Hudson's Bay Company. By the time he joined the Company in 1853, McKay was fluent and literate in English and French, and knew Cree, Ojibwa, Assiniboine, and Sioux dialects. He remained with the company until 1860, being important in negotiating with the Metis and Indians, and was a local expert on transportation. He married Margaret Roward, who inherited substantial money and land. By the late 1860's, McKay had become part of the local landed gentry and built a remarkable home at Deer Lodge on his Assiniboine tract. In later years McKay was a key figure in many Indian treaties. In the 1870's he held several positions in the new Manitoba government. McKay died in 1879, having risen from a Metis odd-job man to a leading businessman, government leader, and a man of tremendous respect in Manitoba.

MCKENZIE, CHARLES

122. Arthur, Elizabeth. CHARLES MCKENZIE, *L'HOMME SEUL*.
Ontario Hist. (Canada) 1978 70(1): 39-62.

A biographical study of Charles McKenzie (1774-1855), clerk to the Hudson's Bay Company at Lac Seul, northwest Ontario, 1807-23 and 1827-54. McKenzie joined the company in 1803; in 1804, he arrived in America, and in 1807 was sent to Lac Seul, a remote, desolate, and impoverished fur trade post. Lacking any influential connections after about 1821, McKenzie failed to secure his promotion or transfer to any more salubrious location. Although his daughters were educated and eventually settled in Upper Canada, he and his half-Indian wife and son were forced to remain at Lac Seul with only brief intervals until 1854. McKenzie wasted much of his energy in fruitless personal quarrels with other neighboring company clerks and factors. Prolonged isolation from European culture, and a growing sense of frustration and failure, tended to warp his judgment. His journals show him to have been a bitter and disillusioned critic of the company's commercial and social policies, and a staunch advocate of fairer treatment of Indians and Metis.

MCNEAL, JOSEPH W.

123. Holmes, Helen Freudenberger. "HE WAS INTO EVERYTHING": JOSEPH W. MCNEAL, TERRITORIAL INNOVATOR.
Chronicles of Oklahoma 1983-84 61(4): 364-385.

Joseph W. McNeal entered Oklahoma as a buffalo hunter during 1873 and over the next 45 years proved his uncanny ability to succeed at a variety of occupations despite his lack of formal education. Initially, McNeal homesteaded near Medicine Lodge, Kansas, but by 1878 he purchased the town's newspaper and subsequently was elected county attorney. In 1883, he started a new bank in Medicine Lodge, a business enterprise he duplicated in Guthrie, Oklahoma, after moving there six years later. McNeal rose to prominence in the Republican Party of Oklahoma Territory, and in 1910 he was the party's unsuccessful gubernatorial candidate. Two years later, he moved to Tulsa, where he remained active in banking and civic life until his death in 1918.

MITCHELL, DAVID DAWSON

124. Verdon, Paul E. DAVID DAWSON MITCHELL: VIRGINIAN ON THE WILD MISSOURI.
Montana 1977 27(2): 2-15.

David Dawson Mitchell (1806-1861) began his career in 1828 when he contracted with the American Fur Company for trade along the Missouri River. Because of his adaptability and business acumen, Mitchell served at a variety of posts as the American Fur Company's traveling troubleshooter for the Upper Missouri Outfit, becoming a full partner in 1835. He left the fur trade in 1840 and served as Superintendent of Indian Affairs at St. Louis between 1841 and 1843. In 1846 he enlisted as a lieutenant colonel in the Missouri Volunteers during the Mexican War. He played a significant part in several campaigns including the capture of Chihuahua. His friendship with Zachary Taylor and Taylor's election to the Presidency in 1848 resulted in Mitchell's restoration as Superintendent of Indian Affairs in St. Louis from 1849 to 1853. His major accomplishment was the Fort Laramie Treaty of 1851. In the remaining years before his death, Mitchell invested in transportation ventures, wrote about his Indian experiences, and helped supply the U.S. Army's 1858 expedition against the Mormons in Utah.

MORTON, THOMAS

125. Gragg, Larry. "THIS TROUBLESOME PLANTER", 1622-46: THOMAS MORTON OF MERRY MOUNT. *Hist. Today (Great Britain) 1977 27(10): 667-672.*

Thomas Morton was a settler among the Puritans in Plymouth Plantation whose trading with Indians and fondness for drink and women caused him to be deported to England twice and imprisoned three times; he founded his own rival community, Merry Mount, and traded furs, liquor, and guns with the local Indians, 1627.

N

NAIRNE, THOMAS

126. Alsop, J. D. THOMAS NAIRNE AND THE "BOSTON GAZETTE NO. 216" OF 1707. *Southern Studies 1983 22(2): 209-211.*

Thomas Nairne was the first provincial Indian agent in South Carolina and an expansionist. In 1708 he was arrested and imprisoned without trial for a year, primarily because of his feud with the governor. However he was charged in a newspaper with being a supporter of the Stuart pretender to the English throne. Nairne denied the charge and attributed it to personal enemies, a story that has been accepted until now along with his innocence. Two letters recently acquired by the British Museum prove Nairne was lying; his alibi against the charges depended on a copy of a newspaper that had not yet been printed.

NATION, CARRY AMELIA

127. Blochowiak, Mary Ann. "WOMAN WITH A HATCHETT": CARRY NATION COMES TO OKLAHOMA TERRITORY.
Chronicles of Oklahoma 1981 59(2): 132-151.

Carry Nation entered the temperance crusade following her 1867 marriage to Charles Gloyd, a hopeless alcoholic. A second marriage led her to Richmond, Texas, where she underwent a religious awakening that fired her crusading enthusiasm. In 1899 she launched her famous "hatchet campaigns" against saloons in Kansas and Oklahoma. Nation's militancy caused various chapters of the Women's Christian Temperance Union to close their doors to her, and she responded to them with venom. Local sheriffs frequently arrested Carry Nation and her following subsided by1906. She died alone and penniless at Leavenworth, Kansas, in 1911.

NEWHOUSE, SAMUEL

128. Rudd, Hynda. SAMUEL NEWHOUSE: UTAH MINING MAGNATE AND LAND DEVELOPER.
Western States Jewish Hist. Q. 1979 11(4): 291-307.

Samuel Newhouse (18554-1930) had a freighting business to mining camps in Colorado, 1879-86, when he made several successful mining investments. He moved to Utah in 1896 as a millionaire investor and developer of mining properties. Newhouse, and his partner Thomas Weir, developed rich copper mines in Bingham Canyon, near Salt Lake City. British investors backed Newhouse and Weir in the 1898 establishment of the Boston Consolidated Copper and Gold Mining Company, Ltd. Fluctuations in the copper market prompted the merger of Boston Consolidated with the Utah Copper Company in 1910. At the same time, Newhouse financed the construction of many large commercial buildings,including a luxury hotel, in Salt Lake City. These investments overextended Newhouse financially, leading to bankruptcy in 1915. Newhouse moved to France to live with his sister in 1920. He died in 1930.

NICHOLAS, CARY

129. Golladay, Dennis. A SECOND CHANGE: CARY NICHOLAS AND FRONTIER FLORIDA.
Florida Historical Quarterly 1985 64(2): 129-147.

After failing in previous career decisions, Cary Nicholas was given a second chance when Florida became an American possession in 1821. His establishment of the *Floridian,* in partnership with George Brooke Tunstall, gave Nicholas political contacts. His life demonstrates how the Florida acquisition opened opportunities to individuals who had failed elsewhere.

NORBY, PETER

130. Arestad, Sverre, ed. QUESTING FOR GOLD AND FURS IN ALASKA.
Norwegian-American Studies 1962 21: 54-94.

Reprints two autobiographical narratives of Norwegian Americans who sought their fortunes in the Klondike area of Alaska. The first, Peter "Yakima Pete" Norby, left his home in Seattle to go to the Klondike in 1897. His narrative relates the life of gold mining towns and offers a detailed account of his trip from Seattle to Klondike City, accompanied by a friend, Fred Jungst. The second narrative is a compilation of two members of the Teien family, Clarence, who was involved in the Alaskan fur trade, and George, who sailed the *Anna-Olga,* a schooner based in Poulsbo, Washington during 1912-16.

NORTON, JOSHUA ABRAHAM ("EMPEROR")

131. McDonald, Michael S. EMPEROR NORTON.
Am. West 1980 17(5): 30-32, 51, 61.

The parents of English-born Joshua Abraham Norton (1819-80) joined a colonizing venture in South Africa. Joshua inherited his father's merchant enterprise but sold out to join the 1849 California gold rush. He became wealthy as a shrewd investor in commodities; but he failed in an attempt to corner the rice market and was forced into bankruptcy in 1856. In a retreat from reality, Norton came to believe that he could save the nation from the disaster of an impending civil war. He issued a proclamation, 17 September 1859, and assumed the title of Norton I, Emperor of the United States. San Franciscans allowed him this illusion, with all of its trappings, for the rest of his life.

NURNBERGER, FREDERICK

132. Prashek, James L. THE NURNBERGERS IN DAKOTA: A FAMILY BIOGRAPHY. *North Dakota Hist. 1979 46(4): 9-19.*

Frederick Nurnberger, native of Germany (b. 1838), arrived in Wisconsin with his parents in 1854. As an adult he moved to North Dakota where he and his numerous progeny became owners of large tracts of land in Richland County. Frederick was director in the Farmers Mutual Protecive Association, was on the Board of Township supervisors, and was elected justice of the peace, getting the reputation of a troublemaker, though always honest and fairdealing. However, in later life, a suit was brought against him for fraudulant manipulation of homestead claims. Drawnout litigation clouded his old age and he died in 1923.

O

OPPENHEIMER, MARCUS

133. Stern, Norton B. MARCUS OPPENHEIMER OF MARCUS, WASHINGTON. *Western States Jewish Hist. Q. 1983 15(4): 334-337.*

In 1862, Marcus Oppenheimer and his brothers, Joseph and Samuel, established a homestead and store on the banks of the Columbia River. They served the placer miners, including many Chinese, as well as the Indians of the region. The major sales items were clothing, groceries, and tobacco; the medium of exchange was gold dust. Besides the store, the Oppenheimer brothers owned a flour mill at Arden, and invested in mining enterprises. The original townsite, named for Marcus Oppenheimer,was inundated by the waters of the Grand Coulee Dam.

P

PAPERMASTER, BENJAMIN

134. Papermaster, Isadore. A HISTORY OF NORTH DAKOTA JEWRY AND THEIR PIONEER RABBI. *Western States Jewish Hist. Q. 1977 10(1): 74-89; 1978 10(2): 170-184, 10(3): 266-283.*

Part I. Rabbi Benjamin Papermaster was born in Lithuania in 1860. He agreed to come to America in 1890 to serve a party of immigrants as its religious leader and teacher. He settled in Grand Forks, North Dakota, amid a growing congregation of Jews from the Ukraine, Rumania, Poland, and Germany. Most of the Jews at that time were peddlers who mortgaged their houses and wagons to build the first synagogue. Rabbi Papermaster was enthusiastic about America; his letters to his family in Lithuania brought many relatives to join him. Grand Forks was considered a boom town because of the building of the Great Northern Railway. The influx of eastern capital helped the development of Jewishmerchants. Part II. Until the turn of the century, Rabbi Papermaster of Grand Forks was the only rabbi serving Jews in all of North Dakota and western Minnesota. Jewish families who started as peddlers became prosperous enough to move out to towns and villages where they opened small shops and stores. Other families followed the Great Northern Railway along its branch lines toward the Canadian border. In Grand Forks, the Jewish community established a modern Hebrew school, a Ladies' Aid Society, and a burial society. Part III. The city of Grand Forks, at the urging of Rabbi Papermaster, acquired a sanitary meat slaughtering facility with a special department for kosher beef. Rabbi Papermaster maintained an active interest in local politics, generally favoring the Republican Party but supporting Democrats when he knew them to be good men. Although a member of a Zionist organization, he worried about the antireligious character of the modern movement. During World War I he urged Jewish youths to their patriotic duty of joining the American armed forces. Rabbi Papermaster died on 24 September 1934.

PENN, WILLIAM

135. Morgan, Edmund S. THE WORLD OF WILLIAM PENN.
Pro. of the Am. Phil. Soc. 1983 127(5): 291-315.

William Penn made his life a testimony against the world in which he lived. He was not content to acquiesce to the social order. Penn wanted to change the world immediately, and he left his mark on it because he did not reject as much of the world as he seemed to; he knew how the world worked and he was prepared to work within its terms. Discusses aspects of Penn's personality as a Protestant, a gentleman, and an Englishman. In regard to Pennsylvania, Penn expected too much both of himself and of those he persuaded to settle. While Quaker spiritual perfection meant self-denial, he was not ready to deny himself privileges and rights that he thought were his perquisites as founder. Further, his colonists seemed equally unwilling to deny themselves anything.

PHILLIPS, LOUIS

136. Stern, Norton B. LOUIS PHILLIPS OF THE POMONA VALLEY: RANCHER AND REAL ESTATE PROMOTER.
Southern California Q. 1983 65(2): 167-195.

Profiles Louis Phillips (1829-1900), one of the wealthiest men in southern California in the latter half of the 19th century. Born in Kempen, Poland, Phillips came to America in 1848 and arrived in Los Angeles in 1851. He bought and successfully operated the San Antonio Rancho. In 1863 Phillips agreed to manage the 12,000-acre San Jose Rancho, comprising what is now the Pomona Valley. He bought the property in 1866 for $30,000. Phillips was known as a successful rancher and real estate investor, respected by the business and financial community for his acumen and integrity. A nonobservant Jew who married a gentile, Phillips maintained close friendships with many members of the Los Angeles Jewish community, a fact overlooked by later generations of Pomona Valley historians. At his death in 1900 Phillips's estate was valued at $1.5 million. The name of this important pioneer is memorialized in Phillips Boulevard in Pomona, the Phillips mansion now under restoration, and other landmarks.

PORTER, SAMUEL (FAMILY)

137. Raymond, Andrew. A NEW ENGLAND COLONIAL FAMILY: FOUR GENERATIONS OF THE PORTERS OF HADLEY, MASSACHUSETTS.
New England Hist. and Genealogical Register 1975 129(July): 198-220.

Recounts the rise of the Porter family to prominence in western Massachusetts. Samuel (d. 1689) was one of the founders of Hadley, but it was the three generations after him—especially his son, Samuel, Jr. (1660-1722), his grandson, Eleazer (1698-1751), and his great-grandsons Eleazer (1728-97) and Elisha (b. 1742)—who took advantage of the benefits of trade, land speculation, military offices, political patronage, and marriage alliances to make the Porters almost, but never quite, the equal of the Connecticut Valley "River Gods." Eleazer's and Elisha's affirmation of the patriot cause in the American Revolution and their adamant opposition to Shays' Rebellion secured for this family its legacy of wealth and political power as the 18th century came to a close.

POST, JUSTUS

138. Foley, William E. JUSTUS POST: PORTRAIT OF A FRONTIER LAND SPECULATOR.
Missouri Hist. Soc. Bull. 1979 36(1): 19-26.

Revisionist historiography treats frontier land speculators kindly, crediting them with civic virtue, business acumen, and beneficial influence on the development of raw frontier communities. Justus Post (1780-1846) was one such benevolent speculator who came to the St. Louis area in 1815. There his quest of personal riches proved less successful than his civic boosting and contributions as public office-holder.

POWELL, JOHN WESLEY

139. Anderson, Martin J. JOHN WESLEY POWELL'S EXPLORATIONS OF THE COLORADO RIVER ... FACT, FICTION, OR FANTASY?
J. of Arizona Hist. 1983 24(4): 363-380.

Demonstrates that John Wesley Powell's famous and influential *Exploration of the Colorado River* (1875) was not a day-to-day diary of his 1869 expedition but was compiled five years later to influence Congress. The hoax reveals Powell as egocentric and self-serving despite his contributions to knowledge of the West.The hoax helped Powell become the director of the US Geological Survey and the Bureau of Ethnology.

PROPST, MISSOURI POWELL

140. Propst, Nell Brown. VOICE FROM THE FRONTIER. *Methodist Hist. 1982 20(2): 51-59.*

Missouri Powell Propst, born in Alabama and a daughter of a sometime Methodist minister, came with her husband to northeastern Colorado in 1874 to participate in taming the frontier. She helped to organize the first Methodist Episcopal Church, South in the area and later tried to serve in a meaningful way with the congregation of the northern Methodist Episcopal Church. When she found that women were used in a very limited way in the church, she sent, in 1891, an article in protest to the *Christian Advocate*. Her article, which was not accepted, is printed here.

Q

QUESENBURY, WILLIAM

141. Benton, Lee David. ON THE BORDER OF INDIAN TERRITORY: THE OKLAHOMA ADVENTURES OF WILLIAM QUESENBURY. *Chronicles of Oklahoma 1984 62(2): 134-155.*

William Quesenbury played a significant role in Southwestern history, especially through his close relationship with the Cherokees. He led Cherokee settlers into Texas during the 1840's, fought in the Mexican War, journeyed to the California goldfields, and published a prominent newspaper at Fayetteville, Arkansas. At the beginning of the Civil War he received a Union appointment as Creek agent, but instead pledged his loyalty to the Confederacy. Quesenbury played a key role in

Albert Pike's treaty mission to the tribes of Indian Territory, and subsequently served as departmental quartermaster for the Confederacy.

RAYMOND, ALMIRA AND WILLIAM WAKEMAN

142. Freeman, Olga, ed. ALMIRA RAYMOND LETTERS, 1840-1880.
Oregon Hist. Q. 1984 85(3): 291-303.

Almira Raymond and her husband, William Wakeman Raymond, sailed from New York in October 1839 and arrived at Fort Vancouver in June 1840, along with other Methodist missionaries for the Pacific Northwest. From their mission stations on the Willamette River and at Tansey Point, she wrote letters to her family, describing their work with the Indians, the physical hardships, illnesses, and loneliness. Later letters speak of their success as Clatsop County dairy farmers and William Raymond's work as an Indian agent.

RED BIRD

143. Zanger, Martin. RED BIRD.
Edmunds, R. David, ed.
American Indian Leaders: Studies in Diversity (Lincoln; U. of Nebraska Pr., 1980): 64-87.

Discusses the Winnebago chief Red Bird and the Winnebago uprising of 1827, labeled the Red Bird Uprising. Red Bird was a local Winnebago leader from western Wisconsin. Although he played only a minor part in the uprising, he surrendered to white authorities. Yet both government officials and white historians have exaggerated his role in the affair, depicting him as the originator of a widespread conspiracy. After his capture he was described in "noble savage" terms by his white captors, who sought to inflate their own importance by increasing the prestige of their foe.

REED, ISAAC

144. Thompson, Donald E. and Sylvester, Lorna Lutes, ed.
THE AUTOBIOGRAPHY OF ISAAC REED, FRONTIER
MISSIONARY.
Indiana Mag. of Hist. 1982 78(3): 193-214.

Isaac Reed served as a Presbyterian missionary and teacher in
Indiana, Kentucky, Illinois, and Ohio from the late 1820's until
the mid-1850's. This portion of his diary covers 1828-39 and
1844-45 and concentrates on his activities of founding many
churches, teaching several frontier schools, and working for the
establishment of many small colleges and seminaries in these
states. The diary entries emphasize his professional life and the
recurring physical ailments he suffered.

REED, ORA EDDLEMAN

145. Morrison, Daryl. *TWIN TERRITORIES: THE INDIAN
MAGAZINE AND ITS EDITOR, ORA EDDLEMAN REED.*
Chronicles of Oklahoma 1982 60(2): 136-166.

Twin Territories: The Indian Magazine represented Oklahoma's
first popular magazine, and from December 1898 to May 1904 it
promoted the virtues and economic possibilities of that region.
Edited by 18-year-old Ora Eddleman, the publication began
operation at Muskogee. Although it changed location several
times, the journal never deviated from its original goal of
praising the territory's Five Civilized Tribes and their
progressive response to the new ways. After her marriage in
1904, Ora Eddleman Reed continued her journalistic work in
Kansas City, Casper, Wyoming, and Tulsa, Oklahoma. Being
part Cherokee, she represented her people well throughout a
lifetime.

REED, SIMEON GANNETT

146. Peterson, Richard H. SIMEON GANNETT REED AND
THE BUNKER HILL AND SULLIVAN: THE
FRUSTRATIONS OF A MINING INVESTOR.
Idaho Yesterdays 1979 23(3): 2-8.

Simeon G. Reed was an Oregon businessman who made a fortune investing in general merchandising, steamboat transportation, and railroads. One of his less successful investments was the purchase of the Bunker Hill and Sullivan Mine in 1887. This lead-silver mine, in Idaho near Coeur d'Alene, was not profitable during Reed's ownership. Reed had trouble finding a competent, experienced superintendent. He was plagued with high railroad freight rates and with lawsuits contesting the property title. Reed sold the mine in 1892.

REES, JOHN

147. Wilks, Ivor G. Hughes. INSURRECTIONS IN TEXAS AND WALES: THE CAREERS OF JOHN REES. *Welsh Hist. Rev. (Great Britain) 1982 11(1): 67-91.*

Suggests that a Welshman, John Rees, who fought in the revolutionary army of Texas in 1835, was the same man who helped organize the Newport insurrection of 1839. Rees volunteered in New Orleans with the 2nd Company of the Greys, participated in the successful siege of Bexar, November 1835, was captured by the Mexicans, and sentenced to death. He escaped, claimed a land bounty from the Texas Republic, was discharged, and sold his entitlements. In the meantime, he had almost certainly been the operational commander of John Frost's workers' army in the attack on Newport, Wales, in 1839. Rees fled to Texas after the attack failed. Although the Melbourne administration succeeded in minimizing the Newport insurrection, the truth is that several thousand men participated and were led by a man who also had fought in the Texan struggle against Mexico.

REID, BERNARD J.

148. Gordon, Mary McDougall. "THIS ITALY AND GARDEN SPOT OF ALL-AMERICA": A FORTY-NINER'S LETTERS FROM THE SANTA CLARA VALLEY IN 1851. *Pacific Historian 1985 29(1): 4-16.*

Narrates the experiences of Bernard J. Reid, a forty-niner from western Pennsylvania, who wrote letters about his adventures in California during 1849-52. Like thousands of goldseekers, his time in the goldfields was one of bewilderment and defeat, accustomed as he was to the comforts of home and the luxuries of a civilized life. One venture after another ended in Reid being further in debt, especially to Walter Hawxhurst, who accompanied him on the overland journey. Reid's last year in California, spent in the Santa Clara Valley, exposed him to a lifestyle in great contrast to the social chaos of the lawless mining settlements where he initially settled.

REISDORFF, JOSEPH

149. Weaver, Bobby D. FATHER JOSEPH REISDORFF: CATHOLIC COLONIZER OF THE PLAINS. *Panhandle-Plains Hist. Rev. 1983 56: 127-140.*

Father Joseph Reisdorff played a key role in the development of northwestern Texas, both as a Catholic priest and as a promoter of German-Catholic colonies. In 1891, he helped establish Windthorst south of Wichita Falls, and over the next 31 years he repeated the feat by organizing the communities of Rhineland, Wynne, Nazareth, Umbarger, Putnam, and Slaton. Each community still retains an extremely faithful Catholic orientation and the outward vestiges of German culture.

RHODES, MARY W. K. D.

150. Pister, M. Claire. MARY. *Pacific Hist. 1980 24(3): 325-343.*

Mary W. K. D. Rhodes (13 October 1808-16 September 1893), the author's great-grandmother, was born and educated in New Hampshire. She was a teacher; when widowed in the 1830's in Charleston, South Carolina, she resumed teaching. In 1838 she married Colonel Elisha Rhodes and moved to Galveston Island, Texas. Her husband was the US Consul to the Republic of Texas. When he was ill or away, she took care of his business. When Colonel Rhodes became an invalid in 1848, Mary took over running the family of his, her, and their children. For financial reasons she went to California alone in 1850, set up a boarding house in San Francisco, and bought some property in Stockton. The family was brought west, where its fortunes went up and down. Mary built Windsor Farm in Stockton. Mary supported the South in the Civil War and lost her two younger sons in that conflict. She left the farm to Stark Blount Smith, Jr., her grandson who had cared for her and the farm.

RICHARDSON, JAMES

151. Hamblen, Charles F. A PIONEER FAMILY: THE RICHARDSONS OF MOUNT DESERT. *Maine Hist. Soc. Q. 1976 16(1): 20-28.*

Traces the migration of James Richardson and his family from Gloucester, Massachusetts, to the Deer Isle-Mount Desert region in Maine in 1761. Notes their struggles for survival on the Maine frontier, the arrival of the Someses, Thurstons, Gotts, and Hamblens in the 1760's and 1770's, and their establishment of a Committee of Correspondence, Safety, and Inspection in 1776.

RICKETTS, WILLIAM "BIG BILL"

152. Neal, Linda Ricketts. WILLIAM RICKETTS: PEACEKEEPER ON THE TOWN FRONTIER, 1896-1922. *Ann. of Iowa 1975 43(1): 62-78.*

From 1896 to 1922, William "Big Bill" Ricketts (1867-1922) alternated between serving as town marshal of Ames and sheriff of Story County. Although it was the home of Iowa State Agricultural College, Ames was a relatively small community when Ricketts became marshal—the town's only law officer. Describes Rickett's daily routine and his work in solving several major crimes. Ricketts was a figure of stability in a time of transition for Ames and Story County.

RIEL, LOUIS

153. Flanagan, Thomas. LOUIS RIEL AND THE DISPERSION OF THE AMERICAN METIS. *Minnesota History 1985 49(5): 179-190.*

Louis Riel, leader of the Red River Rebellion in Manitoba during 1869-70, left the US Red River settlements in 1880 with one hundred other part Indian, part French Metis for Montana, to where Metis had been migrating throughout the 1870's. Riel's band unsuccessfully sought a land grant from the US government, and subsequently scattered, some going to reservations, some living as white homesteaders. This differed from the Canadian practice, whereby recognition of the Metis as a distinct group allowed the Metis to attain land from the government as Metis.

ROSS, JOHN

154. Moulton, Gary E. JOHN ROSS.
Edmunds, R. David, ed.
American Indian Leaders: Studies in Diversity (Lincoln: U. of Nebraska Pr., 1980): 88-106.

Although only one-eighth Cherokee by blood, John Ross fought to keep the Cherokee Indians from being removed from their homes in Georgia and Tennessee to present-day Oklahoma. Although Ross's efforts failed, he continued to serve the tribe as "principal chief" during the post-removal and Civil War period. His diplomatic efforts were severely impeded by the factionalism which existed in many of the tribes, and the inability of tribal leaders to unify their people.

ROWLANDSON, MARY WHITE

155. Greene, David L. NEW LIGHT ON MARY ROWLANDSON.
Early American Literature 1985 20(1): 24-38.

Argues that Mary Rowlandson, the Lancaster, Massachusetts, resident who wrote the first Indian captivity narrative after being captured during King Philip's War during the mid 1670's, was born in 1637, not 1635. Rowlandson did not die in 1678 as previously believed, but in 1711 in Connecticut.

ROWLEY, GRAHAM AND DIANA

156. Labreche, Julianne. HUSBAND AND WIFE BOTH ARE ARCTIC AUTHORITIES.
Can. Geographic (Canada) 1980 101(1): 70-75.

Since archaeologist, explorer, military man, and senior federal scientific advisor Graham Rowley first explored Baffin Island in

1936, studying the archaeological sites of the Dorset and Thule peoples, he and his wife, archaeologist and editor Diana Rowley, have been interested in the Arctic; 1936-81.

ROZENSTAIN, YAEL

157. Rozenstain, Yael. MEMOIRS OF AN ALASKAN MERCHANT.
Western States Jewish Hist. Q. 1977 9(3): 253-261.

The author left Russia as a boy of 12 in 1900. He worked as a cabin boy on an English ship, and as a peddler in Australia until 1906 when he came to the United States. Joining the gold rush to Alaska, he became an apprentice in a general store in Fairbanks, later opening his own business and following the placer miners from one mining camp to another. After World War I, he bought a lot and built a store in the mining town of Hyder in southern Alaska. The decline of the mining industry forced him to move to the big fishing camp at Dillingham in 1938. The fishing business proved too risky for Rozenstain. He sold his outfit in 1944 and retired to southern California.

RUSBY, HENRY HURD

158. Bender, George A. HENRY HURD RUSBY: SCIENTIFIC EXPLORER, SOCIETAL CRUSADER, SCHOLASTIC INNOVATOR.
Pharmacy in Hist. 1981 23(2): 71-85.

Dr. Henry Hurd Rusby (1855-1940) was professor (1888-1930) and dean (1905-30) of the College of Pharmacy of the City of New York (later the Columbia University College of Pharmacy), a botanist and pharmacognosist with Parke-Davis and a consultant to other pharmaceutical manufacturers, and an explorer of considerable repute in North and South America. Rusby's five expeditions from the 1880's to the 1920's uncovered the sources of a great variety of new vegetable drugs, many of which were accepted into the practice of pharmacy and medicine as evidenced by the US Pharmacopoeia (USP) and National Formulary entries, and other plant products with economic possibilities. During 30 years as a member of the Committee on Revision of the USP and in his research and publications, Rusby steadfastly maintained a concern for the standards of vegetable drug sources and the manufacturing and distributional quality of these drugs. He was often critical of the positions taken by government scientists and bureaucrats, pharmaceutical manufacturers, and even other physicians.

RUST, HORATIO NELSON

159. Chaput, Donald. HORATIO N. RUST AND THE AGENT-AS-COLLECTOR DILEMMA.
Southern California Q. 1982 64(4): 281-295.

Describes how Horatio N. Rust (1828-1906), successful businessman and civic leader, used his position as agent to the Mission-Thule Consolidated Agency, during 1889-93, to collect Indian artifacts and pursue his interest in archaeology. A controversial Indian agent, Rust opposed Catholic missionary efforts and took sides in reservation politics. But the biggest dispute about his work centered on his collecting Indian artifacts, a life-long obsession for which agency work provided great opportunities. Rust was criticized for taking objects without paying for them and then selling them at huge profits. Rust amassed several large collections and sold them to museums and schools, unlike other contemporary collectors who donated their collections. Rust took advantage of his position as Indian agent to satisfy his obsession, failing to realize how this action offended public sensibilities.

S

SACAGAWEA

160. Schroer, Blanche. BOAT-PUSHER OR BIRD WOMAN? SACAGAWEA OR SACAJAWEA?
Ann. of Wyoming 1980 52(1): 46-54.

Investigates the debate inaugurated by Grace Raymond Hebard during the 1920's and 1930's that an Indian woman named Porivo was the original Sacagawea who had accompanied the 1804-06 Lewis and Clark Expedition. Evidence indicates that Porivo, who died on Wyoming's Wind River Reservation in 1884, was not Sacagawea, although she may have encountered the original Sacagawea (who died in 1812) or heard stories of her exploits. Anna Lee Waldo's *Sacajawea* (New York: Avon, 1979) adopts the improbable Porivo theme and creates an even more improbable story loosely based on Porivo's life.

SANDERSON, GEORGE WILLIAM

161. Sanderson, George William; Spry, Irene M., ed. THE ETHNIC VOICE: THE "MEMORIES" OF GEORGE WILLIAM SANDERSON, 1846-1936.
Canadian Ethnic Studies (Canada) 1985 17(2): 115-134.

Presents the personal narrative of an English-speaking Metis. Born on Hudson Bay in 1846, George William Sanderson grew up in pioneer Portage la Prairie. After an abortive apprenticeship to a miller, he became a Plains trader and then a farmer, first near Minnedosa and then west of Prince Albert, where he combined farming with freighting until the railway came. He died in 1936. His life exemplifies the traumatic transition from the days of the fur trade and buffalo hunt to settled agriculture. He was imprisoned in Fort Garry in 1870 and encountered difficulties in connection with the Riel uprising in 1885. His memoirs give a vivid impression of the character and concerns of a Prince Rupert's Land family and friends.

SATANTA

162. Worcester, Donald. SATANTA.
Edmunds, R. David, ed.
American Indian Leaders: Studies in Diversity (Lincoln: U. of Nebraska Pr., 1980): 107-130.

Satanta (Set-tainte, or White Bear) (1820-78), was a notable Kiowa warrior who violently resisted the whites in the struggle for the preservation of his peoples' lands on the southern Great Plains. Ultimately his efforts proved futile. Satanta was jailed repeatedly, and finally committed suicide. To his own people Satanta was a tragic hero, while to whites he was an archenemy.

SCHINDLER, THERESE MARCOT LASALIERE

163. McDowell, John E. THERESE SCHINDLER OF
MACKINAC: UPWARD MOBILITY IN THE GREAT LAKES
FUR TRADE.
Wisconsin Mag. of Hist. 1977-78 61(2): 125-143.

Chooses Therese Marcot Lasaliere Schindler's career to
illustrate that: 1) many successful fur traders enjoyed a high
degree of upward economic and social mobility, 2) some did not
travel seasonally to trade for furs, but worked from permanent
homes, trading hardware and supplies with the same Indian
bands continuously, and 3) a few of the wealthiest fur traders
were women. Other women noted include Madeline La
Framboise and Elizabeth Mitchell. Covers 1775-1855.

SCHOOLCRAFT, HENRY ROWE

164. Bremer, Richard C. HENRY ROWE SCHOOLCRAFT:
EXPLORER IN THE MISSISSIPPI VALLEY, 1818-1832.
Wisconsin Mag. of Hist. 1982 66(1): 40-59.

Although remembered as an early writer on the North American
Indian tribes and the discoverer of Lake Itasca, Schoolcraft,
during his 14 years of travel, also served as a member of a
number of government-sponsored expeditions of the Upper
Mississippi Valley, wrote books establishing himself as a
scientific observer, and, finally, "became a traveling exponent of
the evangelization of the Indian."

SEASHORE, CARL EMIL

165. Linton, S. J. THE MAN AND THE MIND: CARL
EMIL SEASHORE, A PIONEER ON TWO FRONTIERS.
Swedish Pioneer Hist. Q. 1980 31(2): 122-128.

Carl Emil Seashore (1866-1949) was born in Morlunda,
Sweden, and came to America with his parents in 1869.
Describes their frontier life in Boone County, Iowa. After
attaining the PhD in Philosophy at Yale in 1895, he returned to
Iowa and founded a school of psychology at the University of
Iowa. He later became the dean of the Graduate School. In 1911

he was elected president of the American Psychological Association.

SEYMOUR, JAMES

166. Robertson, Heard. THE REVEREND JAMES SEYMOUR, FRONTIER PARSON, 1771-1783. *Hist. Mag. of the Protestant Episcopal Church 1976 45(2): 145-153.*

During 1771-81 James Seymour was rector of St. Paul's Parish, Augusta, Georgia. He was an avowed loyalist. Delineates the difficulties this obstinate man faced during the American Revolution and the terrible cost in deprivation of property and position and separation from family which he paid.

SHEFTALL, LEVI

167. Stern, Malcolm H. GROWING UP IN PIONEER SAVANNAH: THE UNFINISHED MEMOIR OF LEVI SHEFTALL (1739-1809). *Michael: On the Hist. of the Jews in the Diaspora (Israel) 1975 3: 15-22.*

Levi Sheftall was a son of Benjamin Sheftall (1692-1765), a native of Prussia and one of the first Jews to settle in Georgia; he was half-brother to Mordecai Sheftall. Reprints the oldest known memoir of an American Jew and possibly the earliest description of life in pioneer Savannah. Starting from scratch, Levi Sheftall accumulated a large fortune, including many slaves, but eventually lost most of it. Imprisoned as a rebel during the American Revolution, he denied entertaining such sentiments. He was active in Jewish community life.

SHIVELY, JOHN M.

168. List, Howard M. and List, Edith M., ed. JOHN M. SHIVELY'S MEMOIR. *Oregon Hist. Q. 1980 81(1): 4-29, (2): 180-195.*

Part I. John M. Shively (1804-93), Oregon pioneer, recorded his reminiscences in 1883. Describes some family background, his experiences on his way to Oregon in 1843, his stay in Astoria, and the beginning of his trip back East in 1845. Describes problems with Indians.Part II. Conclusion. Shively's adventures from 1845 to 1851 included advising the government on the Oregon situation during 1845-46, being the first postmaster west of the Rocky Mountains (in Astoria, Oregon), organizing the Pacific mail service, and participating in the California gold rush.

SHORB, JAMES DE BARTH

169. Sherwood, Midge. JAMES DE BARTH SHORB: A MAN AHEAD OF HIS TIME, 1842-1896. *Southern California Quarterly 1984 66(4): 287-302.*

Profiles James De Barth Shorb, pioneer viticulturist and land developer in the San Gabriel Valley of Southern California. Born in Maryland, Shorb moved to California in 1864, participated in oil exploration, and married a daughter of pioneer Benjamin D. Wilson. Shorb became Wilson's business associate, founded the San Gabriel Wine Company, and was involved in many activities, including establishing the community of Alhambra. A man of vision and integrity, Shorb died prematurely while fighting a blight that attacked his vineyards. Many of his ideas, however, were eventually realized by those who followed him. The Huntington Library is located on land once owned by Shorb.

SIEBEN, HENRY

170. Pace, Dick. HENRY SIEBEN: PIONEER MONTANA STOCKMAN. *Montana 1979 29(1): 2-15.*

Henry Sieben (1847-1937) came to Montana's gold fields in 1864, was a farm laborer, prospector, and freighter, then turned to livestock raising along the Smith River in 1870. In partnership with his brothers Leonard and Jacob, Henry Sieben raised cattle and became one of the territory's pioneer sheep ranchers in 1875. The partnership was dissolved in 1879 and Henry moved his stock to the Lewistown area. He established a reputation as an excellent businessman and as someone who took care of his stock and employees. After ranching in the

Culbertson area, Henry Sieben purchased ranches near Cascade and along Little Prickly Pear Creek, forming the Sieben Livestock Company. By 1907, these two ranches had become the heart of his cattle and sheep raising business which he directed from his home in Helena.Sieben became well known for his business approach to ranching and for his public and private philanthropies. His family continues to operate the Sieben Ranch Company today.

SIMPSON, GEORGE

171. Johnson, Stephen M. WRANGEL AND SIMPSON.
Judd, Carol M. and Ray, Arthur J., ed.
Old Trails and New Directions: Papers of the Third North American Fur Trade Conference (Toronto: U. of Toronto Pr., 1980): 207-216.

Details the rivalry and friendship between Baron Ferdinand von Wrangel, the governor of the Russian-American Company, and George Simpson, governor of the Hudson's Bay Company, which began in 1834 over a confrontation between the two companies and lasted until the early 1840's. They worked with each other in the late 1830's and early 1840's to develop and expand their contract agreement, which was a result of the earlier conflict, and which gave a breath of life to the troubled Russian colony and also gave the Hudson's Bay Company some control over its last competitor on the continent. Had Wrangel not confronted the Hudson's Bay Company, the British company probably would have driven the Russians off the coast and absorbed Russian America into their fur trade empire. Thus Wrangel and Simpson's relationship in effect prolonged the existence of the Russian colony in Alaska.

SMART, WILLIAM HENRY

172. Rogers, Kristen Smart. WILLIAM HENRY SMART: UINTA BASIN PIONEER LEADER.
Utah Hist. Q. 1977 45(1): 61-74.

William Henry Smart (1862-1937) was a classic example of the severe, disciplined, dedicated men who built Utah. He organized and lead the settlement of Utah's Uinta Basin. He organized realty companies, financed needed businesses and civic enterprises, promoted schools, banks, and newspapers. He gave so freely of his wealth to establish Mormon rule in the Basin that he left there almost penniless. The Uinta Basin bears unmistakably the stamp of his labors.

SMART, WILLIAM H.

173. WILLIAM H. SMART, BUILDER IN THE BASIN.
Utah Hist. Q. 1982 50(1): 59-67.

Philanthropist and successful rancher-businessman, William H. Smart built and donated land (and his money) to the erection of the Uintah Telephone Company in Vernal (1907) and established the towns of Duchesne, Myton, Randlett (all in 1905), and Roosevelt (1906). Land for Wasatch High School was given by Smart. To encourage investment, he personally used his own resources (never requiring others to repay after repeated losses). Promoted within the Mormon Church, Smart always, as recounted by his grandson, believed he was serving his church and extended his philanthropy for the good of the community.

SMITH, ANDREW JACKSON

174. Jones, Walter L. GROWING UP IN THE
FLATWOODS: JACK SMITH'S MEMORIES OF THE 1860S.
J. of Mississippi Hist. 1980 42(2): 145-151.

Andrew Jackson Smith was born in 1858 in Pontotoc County, Mississippi. Smith's account preserves memories of his father's return from the Civil War in 1864 as well as military skirmishes near his home. He describes the family's home and rural life, educational pursuits, and activities of the Shady Grove Baptist Church. Smith's observations of medical practices, death, and activities around the southern country store preserve an interesting picture of life in the Mississippi flatwoods.

SMITH, DONALD A.

175. Morton, W. L. DONALD A. SMITH AND
GOVERNOR GEORGE SIMPSON.
Beaver (Canada) 1978 309(2): 4-9.

Donald A. Smith, the future Baron Strathcona and Mount Royal, was born in Scotland. He came to the Hudson's Bay Company as a minor clerk in the 1830's. In his first several decades he worked at Tadoussac, Labrador, and Esquimeaux Bay. Smith began his career as a sloppy, disorganized bookkeeper, a point emphasized in some of George Simpson's letters to him. However, though Simpson scolded Smith, he challenged him frequently, such as having him head a relief expedition to Labrador in 1848. Over the years, Smith profitted from Simpson's advice, so much so that he later became a director of the Company and was created a baron.

SMITH, JOHN GUY

176. Smith, Jack E. STORY OF A FARMER: A PORTRAIT OF THE LIFE AND FAMILY OF J. GUY SMITH. *Colorado Heritage 1982 1(1): 52-63.*

The author describes the career of his grandfather, John Guy Smith (1854-1937), who moved to Colorado in 1878 for health reasons. His diary during his first year in Colorado describes working on a ranch, in a shoe store, for the railroad, and prospecting. In 1881 he began acquiring land in what is now Denver. He and his brother, George, pioneered irrigation as truck gardeners for some 45 years, and J. Guy was known as the "Celery King" of Colorado. He became a leading citizen and, beginning in 1906, was a member of the Denver board of supervisors, serving for a time as its president. His career was similar to many others, but it illustrates early economic, political, and social history of a frontier state.

SMITH, JOHN W.

177. Gray, John S. THE FRONTIER FORTUNES OF JOHN W. SMITH. *Ann. of Wyoming 1979 51(2): 36-53.*

John W. Smith arrived at Ft. Laramie, Wyoming, in 1857 and joined in a trading enterprise with three partners. During the next 20 years, Smith lived and traded with Indian tribes, and periodically scouted for the Army. He served as field sutler for George Custer's 1874 Black Hills Expedition and wrote accounts of the trip for newspapers. Smith subsequently was sutler at several military posts on the Northern Plains. By the early 1880's, he was able to settle down to a comfortable life in Miles City, Montana. Financial problems overwhelmed him during the following decades, and he died a pauper in 1904 or 1905.

SMITH, MARY FIELDING

178. Andersen, Lavina Fielding. MARY FIELDING SMITH: HER OX GOES MARCHING ON. *Dialogue 1981 14(4): 91-100.*

Mary Fielding Smith, a heroic figure from early Mormon history or folklore, has served as a role model for countless girls and women since the late 19th century. According to Mormon lore, Mary Fielding Smith exercised great religious faith and healed an ox. This enabled her to continue her journey to the Salt Lake Valley in the late 1840's. Although the historical evidence is hazy, the story has survived. For some individuals, particularly women, this pioneer woman has been placed on a pedestal almost unreachable for all but the most devout.

SMITH, NATHAN

179. Wirthlin, LeRoy S. JOSEPH SMITH'S BOYHOOD OPERATION: AN 1813 SURGICAL SUCCESS. *Brigham Young U. Studies 1981 21(2): 131-154.*

Describes the development of surgery in America from 1813 to the present, including a discussion of the work of Dr. Nathan Smith (1762-1829), respected surgeon and professor of surgery at Dartmouth College Medical School, Hanover, New Hampshire, and later at Yale Univerity, who performed leg surgery on Joseph Smith, Mormon founder, when Joseph was seven. Gives a comprehensive, illustrated description of the operation called a sequestrectomy for the treatment of osteomyelitis as performed by Nathan Smith. Although he performed many sequestrectomies, the detailed account of Lucy Mack Smith, Joseph's mother, provides one of Smith's few well-documented total successes with this operation.

SOASH, WILLIAM PULVER

180. Gracy, David B., II. SELLING THE FUTURE: A BIOGRAPHY OF WILLIAM PULVER SOASH. *Panhandle-Plains Hist. Rev. 1977 50: 1-75.*

William Pulver Soash (1877-1961) during 1905-43 helped open the Texas Panhandle to agricultural settlement. His initial colonization efforts were thwarted by the drought of 1909-10, but Soash reorganized his efforts in the southern Panhandle by cooperating with the railroads and large ranchers. Combining humanitarianism with the businessman's instinct for profits, he defied the negative stereotype so often associated with land agents.

SOLOMONS, THEODORE

181. Sargent, Shirley. THEODORE SOLOMONS, AN UNLIKELY MOUNTAINEER. *Western States Jewish History 1986 18(3): 195-203.*

A sketch of the life of Theodore Solomons, who uncovered the first continuous route along the crest of the High Sierra (1892-96), and later spent a decade mountaineering in Alaska. Solomons was the son of Seixas Solomons, a California accountant, and Hannah Marks Solomons.

SPERRY-STEELE, FANNIE

182. Stiffler, Liz and Blake, Tona. FANNIE SPERRY-STEELE: MONTANA'S CHAMPION BRONC RIDER. *Montana 1982 32(2): 44-57.*

Fannie Sperry-Steele rode in the professional rodeo and wild west show circuit from 1907 to 1925. Born on a Montana ranch, Fannie Sperry won the bucking horse contest in 1912 at the Calgary Stampede and became known as Montana's champion bronc rider. In 1913 she married Bill Steele; they toured together until 1925, and from then until 1965 she managed a dude ranch in the Lincoln, Montana area. Discusses the Sperry-Steele family and its professional activities.

SPIEGELBERG, FLORA LANGERMANN

183. Lawson, Michael L. FLORA LANGERMANN
SPIEGELBERG: GRAND LADY OF SANTA FE.
Western States Jewish Hist. Q. 1976 8(4): 291-308.

In 1875 Flora Langermann Spiegelberg (1857-1943) and her
husband Willi (1844-1929) moved to Santa Fe. Willi and his
five brothers operated a wholesale business that, along with new
family enterprises, dominated the economy of the Southwest for
several years. In 1893, the now wealthy Spiegelberg family
moved to New York City. "Garbage Can Flora" became
involved in the movement to clean up the city and she
campaigned for investigations of war profits in the munitions
industry during World War I. In 1914, she helped organize the
Metropolitan Protective Association to work for improved
wages for the city street cleaners. After Willi died she donated
many family items to the Museum of New Mexico.

STAPLETON, PATIENCE TUCKER

184. Dalton, Joann. PATIENCE STAPLETON: A
FORGOTTEN FRONTIER WRITER.
Colorado Mag. 1976 53(3): 261-276.

Sketches the life of Patience Tucker Stapleton and emphasizes
her years in Denver during 1882-93. Born and educated in the
East, she arrived in Denver in 1882 and worked for local
newspapers. A supporter of woman suffrage, she wrote
"newspaper articles, short stories, poems and novels" that
reflected her personal conflicts and her optimism for the West.

STARR, CALEB

185. Lockwood, Patricia W. THE LEGACY OF CALEB
STARR.
Chronicles of Oklahoma 1983 61(3): 288-307.

Caleb Starr was a white man who married into the Cherokee
tribe during the 1790's, established a profitable plantation in
Tennessee, and became important in tribal politics. In 1838, he
moved his family to eastern Indian Territory to escape the
inevitable pressure of forced removal by the federal

government. Starr and his sons were associated with the Old Settler and Treaty Party factions that willingly undertook migration. Arrayed against them was the John Ross faction that resisted removal until forced into Indian Territory. Killings of Starr relatives and others drove the factions further apart until temporary peace was established in 1846.

STEFANSSON, VILHJALMUR

186. Finnie, Richard Sterling. MY FRIEND STEFANSSON. *Alaska J. 1978 8(1): 18-25, 84-85.*

In 1931 the author met Vilhjalmur Stefansson (1879-1962), Canadian-born Arctic explorer and researcher. The author worked under him during World War II for the Office of the Coordinator of Information, which later became the OSS and much later the CIA. Having a brilliant intellect, Stefansson finished a four-year arts program at the State University of Iowa in one year, and later developed the very rare skill of speaking one of the Eskimo languages correctly as well as fluently. He made a few enemies, for example Roald Amundsen, who denounced him as a charlatan, but in general he was and is highly respected as an Arctic expert and pioneer.

STONEBERG, PHILIP J.

187. Ijams, Ethel W. PHILIP J. STONEBERG AND THE PRESERVATION OF BISHOP HILL. *Swedish-American Historical Quarterly 1985 36(1): 26-38.*

Bishop Hill, Illinois, a religious communistic settlement founded by Eric Janson and his Swedish followers, flourished during 1846-61 and is now being preserved as a National Historic Landmark. Philip J. (christened Jonas Philip) Stoneberg (1875-1919) was the grandson of colonists Jonas and Anna Stoneberg. Although he received degrees from Knox College and Columbia and Harvard universities, he spent his career in Bishop Hill as an educator and local historian. He collected documents, reminiscences, and oral histories of the settlement, wrote papers on its history, and delivered historical orations at pioneer celebrations.

STOWE, CALVIN ELLIS

188. Hilgert, Earle. CALVIN ELLIS STOWE: PIONEER LIBRARIAN OF THE OLD WEST. *Lib. Q. 1980 50(3): 324-351.*

Calvin E. Stowe, professor and librarian at Lane Seminary in Cincinnati from 1833 to 1850, was chiefly responsible for the development there of what apparently was the largest academic library in the West. Stowe's contributions extended not only to collection building but also to a heightened sense of the importance of student use of library resources. This article, based largely on manuscript materials, identifies factors that contributed to Stowe's understanding of librarianship, traces the development of the Lane library, and seeks to evaluate his contributions.

STRAHORN, CARRIE ADELL GREEN

189. Cochran, Barbara. DELL STRAHORN—A PIONEER WITH STYLE. *Pacific Northwesterner 1983 27(4): 49, 51-55.*

Traces the lives of Carrie Adell Green Strahorn and her husband, Robert Edmund Strahorn, during their six years of public-relations trips throughout the Northwest for Union Pacific; in later years, they lived in Idaho Territory and in Spokane, where Robert Strahorn was a pioneer developer.

STRANGE, HENRY

190. Walker, Evalyn Capps. THE STRANGE STORY. *Colorado Mag. 1977 54(3): 294-311.*

The author's grandparents, Henry and Susannah Strange, were married in 1850, migrated from England to America in 1855, probably under Mormon auspices, and in 1859 started for Salt Lake City. They got as far as Fort Bridger but returned to St. Joseph. From 1863 until their deaths in 1908 and 1912 they lived in various frontier Colorado communities. Describes the life of Walker's father, Samuel J. Capps, likewise an English immigrant.

STURGEON, SALLIE LEWIS

191. Crockett, Bernice Norman. "NO JOB FOR A WOMAN."
Chronicles of Oklahoma 1983 61(2): 148-167.

Sallie Lewis Sturgeon came to Oklahoma in 1894 with her husband, and they soon established residence in Ardmore. There Mrs. Sturgeon became a reporter for the local newspaper and created a weekly "women's news column." She later began publishing *The Oklahoma Lady,* the first exclusively women's journal published in Oklahoma. Despite her own sense of independence in the business world, Mrs. Sturgeon campaigned against women's suffrage. In 1920, Governor J. B. A. Robertson appointed her as the first female member of the Oklahoma State Health Department's team of sanitary inspectors. She diligently carried out her inspector duties and won praise throughout the state.

STUTE, HEINRICH WILHELM

192. Ira, Alfred; Grimm, A. Ira, transl. PASTOR STUTE IN LANGLADE COUNTY.
Concordia Hist. Inst. Q. 1980 53(4): 172-178.

Relates incidents from the life of Pastor Heinrich Wilhelm Stute as he ministered periodically to the frontier Lutheran community in Langlade County, Wisconsin, during 1887-91.

SUBLETTE, SOLOMON PERRY

193. Sunder, John E. SOLOMON PERRY SUBLETTE: MOUNTAIN MAN OF THE FORTIES.
New Mexico Hist. Rev. 1961 36(1): 49-61.

Recounts the life of Solomon Perry Sublette (1815-57), which is representative of the mountain men of the western states, who trapped, traded, explored, and lived off the land.

SUTTER, JOHN AUGUSTUS

194. Dillon, Richard. VISIONARY AND VICTIM: CAPTAIN JOHN AUGUSTUS SUTTER. *Am. West 1980 17(3): 4-11, 55-59.*

A German born of Swiss extraction, John Augustus Sutter (1803-80) fled the likelihood of debtor's prison and moved to America, where he dabbled with mixed success in the Santa Fe and Oregon country fur trade. He established Sutter's Fort in California's Sacramento Valley. The discovery of gold at his sawmill about 50 miles up in the Sierra foothills triggered the 1849 gold rush and the collapse of his enterprise. Sutter spent his last years on a meager state pension attempting to get recognition and relief from Congress. He was a prepossessing imposter whose outward appearance covered an inner turmoil of hesitancy and passivity.

SUYDAM, NELLIE

195. Bohem, Hilda. NELLIE SUYDAM OF GLENDORA: DIARY OF AN ORDINARY WOMAN. *Southern California Quarterly 1984 66(4): 335-344.*

A profile of the life of Nellie Suydam, pioneer resident of Glendora, California. Her family moved to Glendora in 1885; Nellie grew up there, earned a living as a printer, married, and tried running a print shop in Arizona, then separated from her husband and returned to Glendora. Hers was an ordinary life with an important exception: she kept a lifelong diary of her activities, filling 29 volumes with the cares and concerns of an ordinary person whose literary ambitions were never quite realized.

SWISSHELM, JANE GREY

196. McCarthy, Abigail. JANE GREY SWISSHELM: MARRIAGE AND SLAVERY. Stuhler, Barbara and Kreuter, Gretchen, ed. *Women of Minnesota: Selected Biographical Essays (St. Paul: Minnesota Historical Society Pr., 1977): 34-54.*

Jane Grey Swisshelm was born of Scotch-Irish parents on 6 December 1815. She grew up in western Pennsylvania. Precocious, she learned to read and sew very early and became a skilled painter. In 1836, she married James Swisshelm, a prosperous farmer. They were unlike in religion, values, and temperament. The marriage proved difficult; in 1857, Jane took her daughter, left her husband, and moved to St. Cloud, Minnesota. By then, she was a noted journalist, abolitionist, and feminist. In her new home, Swisshelm resumed her newspaper career. She soon became embroiled in political controversy with Sylvanus B. Lowry, the proslavery Democratic political ruler of central Minnesota. Swisshelm's journalistic weapons of ruthless irony and vitriolic satire helped to bring about Lowry's decline. She also reported on the Sioux revolt which terrorized the state, in 1862; she advocated stern reprisals against the Indians. In 1863, Swisshelm went to Washington, D.C., and quickly became involved in Civil War nursing, an occupation which, for the first time, brought her approval and encouragement instead of criticism and controversy.

T

TABOR, HORACE A. W.

197. Smith, Duane A. and Halaas, David Fridtjof. A FIFTY-NINER MINER: THE CAREER OF HORACE A. W. TABOR. *Colorado Heritage 1983 (1-2): 24-33.*

Horace A. W. Tabor came to Colorado in 1859 during the Pikes Peak gold rush. He mined, prospected, and ran a general store in various places. In 1878, he gained fame and fortune as a mineowner and speculator. In 1881, Tabor was elected lieutenant governor and in 1883 served briefly as US senator from Colorado. He divorced his wife and married Elizabeth Bonduel McCourt ("Baby Doe") under peculiar circumstances. His financial ventures failed and by 1896 Tabor was broke. Appointed postmaster of Denver in 1898, he died in 1899.

TAYLOR, JAMES

198. Vitz, Robert C. GENERAL JAMES TAYLOR AND THE BEGINNINGS OF NEWPORT, KENTUCKY. *Filson Club Hist. Q. 1976 50(4): 353-368.*

James Taylor, one of the founders of Newport, Kentucky, was a member of a prominent Virginia family and cousin of President Zachary Taylor. He first settled on his father's Kentucky land in 1793. He soon purchased this and other tracts of land and began to try to attract settlers to the region. Despite the presence of a military garrison, growth was slow until 1830.

TENGGREN, JOHAN FREDRIK

199. Almqvist, Sten; Norton, John E. and Barton, H. Arnold, transl. JOHAN FREDRIK TENGGREN: SOLDIER, POET, GOLD-MINER. *Swedish-American Hist. Q. 1982 33(4): 241-265.*

Johan Fredrik Tenggren was born the son of Lars Wilhelm Tenggren and his wife Gustafva Henrietta Ulrika in 1827. As a youth he displayed a poetic nature, wandering about the Vaxjo area of Sweden, daydreaming, and writing verse. In 1847 he became a volunteer in the Royal Kronoberg Regiment. While serving as a soldier, he composed a marching song for his regiment, and as a result gained occasional contact with the king. In 1851 he resigned the regiment, determined to travel to the gold mines in California. Arriving in New York he traveled to San Francisco via Panama. He was unsuccessful as a miner, but earned a living as an agriculturalist in Stockton, working as a mine laborer in the off-season. He continued to write and publish poetry and returned to his native Sweden in 1866, where he died of a stroke in 1904.

TOOMES, ALBERT

200. Chavez, Thomas E. ALBERT TOOMES, PIN FEATHER ON THE AMERICAN EAGLE. *Pacific Hist. 1978 22(2): 173-183.*

The story of Albert Toomes, one of the original settlers of Tehama, California, touches many of the significant events in the early history of California. A fur trader from Missouri, he received a large grant of land from Mexico in 1844, was a member of the California Dragoons in 1846, and a prospector in 1848, and eventually retired as a wealthy rancher and farmer. His avocations—local organizations, local politics, horse racing, and hunting—were as varied as his occupations.

TRACY, FRANCIS G., SR.

201. Tracy, Francis G., Sr. PECOS VALLEY PIONEERS. *New Mexico Hist. Rev. 1958 33(3): 187-204.*

Reprints the author's reminiscences as a young man who, along with his cousin Joseph S. Stevens and friends J. A. Eddy and C. B. Eddy, was among the early pioneers in New Mexico's Pecos Valley during the late 1880's and early 1890's.

TWITCHELL, AMOS

202. Allison, Hildreth M. DOCTOR AMOS TWITCHELL: PIONEER SURGEON. *Hist. New Hampshire 1978 33(2): 167-179.*

Amos Twitchell (1781-1850), born in Dublin, New Hampshire, studied medicine at Dartmouth, then settled briefly at Marlborough, where he performed the second known ligature of the common carotid artery, on a local militiaman who received an accidental wound in a sham battle in October 1807. Twitchell moved to Keene in 1810, where he added to his reputation by treating victims of an epidemic of spotted fever, and by three successful tracheotomies. Twitchell received many honors in his career.

U

UPSHAW, WILLIAM (FAMILY)

203. Upshaw, Walter E. PIONEERING SPIRIT. *Oregon Hist. Q. 1976 77(4): 369-379.*

Tells about the lives of the author, his father, and their ancestors. William Upshaw, the author's father, always sought a frontier. He raced for land in Oklahoma and won, then farmed coffee in Honduras, and later won another tract of Oklahoma land in a lottery. The family then moved to Oregon, where the author married and began a career somewhat similar to that of his father. Eventually he joined the Department of Agriculture and held a position there for many years.

V

VANN, JOSEPH

204. McFadden, Marguerite. THE SAGA OF "RICH JOE" VANN.
Chronicles of Oklahoma 1983 61(1): 68-79.

Born to a mixed-blood Scottish-Cherokee trading family in 1798, Joseph Vann utilized lucrative family connections to become one of the richest Cherokees. An owner of vast tracts of land, a plantation home, and 110 slaves, he received almost $20,000 from the government for loss of his property during the Cherokee removals. By the late 1830's he had reestablished himself as a wealthy planter near Webbers Falls, Indian Territory, but died in a boating accident in 1844. The Civil War subsequently destroyed most of what Vann bequeathed to his family.

W

WAGNER, WILLIAM (FAMILY)

205. Ammidown, Margot. THE WAGNER FAMILY: PIONEER LIFE ON THE MIAMI RIVER.
Tequesta 1982 42: 5-37.

The Wagner family, from South Carolina, were pioneers in the Miami area, having constructed the oldest known house standing in Miami today. William and Evaline Wagner met, married, and moved to Miami by 1858. Evaline, of mixed blood, was accepted in the area socially, although the members of the Adam Richard family, her daughter's family, were to be persecuted for their darker complexions. Evaline died in 1888; her husband lived until the advent of the 20th century.

WAKELAND, WILLIAM

206. Klein, Janet. WILLIAM WAKELAND: A PIONEER PHOTOGRAPHER IN KACHEMAK BAY.
Alaska J. 1983 13(3): 17-26.

Discusses the works of photographer William Wakeland. As an amateur, Wakeland lived and worked in the Kachemak Bay area of Alaska, photographing the people and the scenery, much of which disappeared in the 1964 earthquake. He captured the essence of the struggle to live in the often harsh environment. An exhibition entitled "William Wakeland: Kachemak Bay Photographs 1946-1953" opened in November 1982 at the Pratt Museum in Homer, Alaska.

WALDO, WILLIAM

207. Goodrich, James W. PROFIT, PHILANTHROPY AND POLITICS: WILLIAM WALDO'S CALIFORNIA YEARS, 1850-1853.
Southern California Q. 1976 58(3): 359-379.

Profiles the California career of William Waldo (1812-81), who at age 37 left his modestly successful business in Missouri to come to California in 1849. Waldo drove cattle on the trip and sold them in the Sacramento area for a good profit; he also invested in Sacramento real estate. Concern over the difficulties experienced on the trail west by immigrants led Waldo to organize a Sacramento relief committee. This committee went up the Truckee River route and into Nevada distributing food and supplies to destitute travelers in 1850. Waldo also expended his personal fortune in this endeavor, but the state legislature reimbursed him $27,000 in 1853. In that year he was the Whig candidate for governor but was narrowly defeated by Democrat John Bigler. Embittered and disappointed by slanders and possible electoral frauds, Waldo left California soon after the election, returning to his family and then moving to Minnesota.

Not a "migratory politician," Waldo came west for economic motives, and his philanthropic efforts were admired by many Californians.

WALES, MARTHA GRAY

208. Wales, Martha Gray and Pope, Willard B., ed. WHEN I WAS A LITTLE GIRL: THINGS I REMEMBER FROM LIVING AT FRONTIER MILITARY POSTS. *North Dakota Hist. 1983 50(2): 12-22.*

Martha Gray Wales's childhood memories of life in military forts on the Dakota frontier. The Indian threat, the loneliness of the frontier, the drudgery of frontier life, and the challenge of the frontier environment were dominant themes of her early experience.

WEBB, JOE

209. Ricker, Neal T. JOE WEBB. *Am. West 1981 18(4): 20-21.*

Joe Webb (1885-1980) drove a Stoddard Stage Lines open stagecoach between Coulterville and Hazel Green, California, 1906-09. He carried tourists as passengers bound for Yosemite National Park and gold destined for the mint in San Francisco. "Stagecoach driving wasn't glamorous at all, just dusty."

WEGG, SAMUEL

210. Ruggles, Richard I. GOVERNOR SAMUEL WEGG: "THE WINDS OF CHANGE." *Beaver (Canada) 1976 307(2): 10-20.*

In 1748, Samuel Wegg inherited some of his father's stock in the Hudson's Bay Company. He accumulated more shares, was elected to the Committee of the Co. in 1760, eventually became governor, and died in 1802. Wegg had a typical gentry upbringing. He became a barrister and joined the right clubs. It was the club affiliations that had an impact on the Company. Wegg for years attended and participated in activities of the Royal Society, the Thursday Club, and the Society of

Antiquaries. He was an intimate of naturalists, cartographers, and explorers; and these interests, coupled with his position with the Company, led to many changes in Hudson's Bay Co. policy and knowledge of geography.

WELLS, WILLIAM

211. Hutton, Paul A. WILLIAM WELLS: FRONTIER SCOUT AND INDIAN AGENT.
Indiana Mag. of Hist. 1978 74(3): 183-222.

A biography of William Wells, a "white Indian" in the Old Northwest who never successfully adapted to the way of life of either group. Captured as a lad, Wells became an Indian, even refusing to reenter white society when the opportunity was offered. He eventually did so, becoming an army scout, Indian agent, farmer, and successful businessman. His facility with Indian languages made him indispensable in the army campaigns of the time, but the breaking of the back of Indian resistance turned his asset into a liability. He squabbled with up-and-coming political figures. Eventually killed in an Indian skirmish, Wells died as he had lived, faithful to the Indian moral code, which was inevitably in conflict with the subtle machinations of the politicians.

212. Hutton, Paul A. THE TWO WORLDS OF WILLIAM WELLS.
Am. Hist. Illus. 1983 28(2): 33-41.

William Wells (1770-1812) was captured in 1784 by Miami Indians in Illinois, fought as a Miami warrior, eventually returned to white society, and then fought against the Indians until his death in 1812.

WHITCOMB, ELIAS W.

213. Whitcomb, Elias W. REMINISCENCES OF A PIONEER: AN EXCERPT FROM THE DIARY OF ELIAS W. WHITCOMB.
Annals of Wyoming 1985 57(2): 21-32.

Elias W. Whitcomb worked as a cattle tender for the famed freighting operation of Russell, Majors, and Waddell during the

1850's, established one of the largest mercantile businesses in Cheyenne, Wyoming, and became one of the first independent landowners in the territory when he purchased ranchlands during 1866. He married Katherine Shaw, daughter of a Scottish trader and a Sioux woman, and they lived a comfortable life in the fashionable "Cattleman's Row" of Cheyenne. Whitcomb's diary relates his experiences with Russell, Majors, and Waddell during the Mormon War of 1858, his association with the notorious Alfred Slade, who was later hanged by vigilantes in Virginia City, Montana, and the frequency of Indian attacks in southeastern Wyoming during the 1860's.

WHITE, EMMET

214. Parks, Annette White, ed. EMMET WHITE: REMINISCENCES OF A RIMROCKER, PART 1. *Oregon Hist. Q. 1984 85(3): 229-252.*

Emmet White was born in Heppner, Oregon, and was raised in the Monument and John Day areas of Grant County. After marriage to Julia Lesley, he ranched in the Monument area until 1947. Stories of family and local history are intertwined: his grandparents, Wallace and Sarah Cochran, were among Monument's first settlers; and his uncle, Emmet Cochran, was a colorful Grant County rancher. Ranching methods changed with the arrival of Mexican and American cowboys (called *vaqueros* or "buckaroos") from California. Each August, the buckaroos drove large herds to the railroad at Winnemucca, Nevada, and Heppner, Oregon.

WICKMILLER, CHARLES PAUL

215. Moss, Genevieve. C. P. "DOC" WICKMILLER: BOOMER WITH A "HATFUL OF PILLS." *Chronicles of Oklahoma 1985 63(2): 192-203.*

Charles Paul Wickmiller joined David L. Payne's illegal "boomers" in their unsuccessful 1883 attempt to stake claims to the unassigned lands of Indian Territory. Six years later, he returned as a legal settler in the "Great Land Run" and his drugstore was the first two-story wooden structure in the fledgling town of Kingfisher. Recognized as an important businessman and civic leader, he was inducted into the

Oklahoma Hall of Fame in 1932. Much of Wickmiller's famed Indian artifact collection was deposited at the Oklahoma Historical Society and Phillips University before his death in 1949.

WILSON, DAVID (FAMILY)

216. Bushman, Claudia. THE WILSON FAMILY IN DELAWARE AND INDIANA.
Delaware Hist. 1982 20(1): 27-49.

Describes the experiences of the Wilson and Corbit families of Odessa, Delaware, as they developed their holdings in farming, tanning, and trade and their subsequent move west to Richmond, Indiana, in the early 19th century. Concludes that the move westward was also a move downward in economic terms and that eastern family members helped to sustain western ones through the first generation, but that over time family bonds weakened and even broke.

WILSON, JOHN

217. Nicholson, Loren. CAPTAIN JOHN WILSON: TRADER OF THE PACIFIC.
Pacific Hist. 1979 23(2): 69-90.

The Scottish-born John Wilson (1798-1861) enjoyed unusual success in trade and land, and much recognition in Alta, California. Describes his many business transactions and partnerships, and his marriage to a Mexican, Ramona, which provided him entry into Mexican California. He was, with his partners, the largest landholder in what is now San Luis Obispo County. Through the education of her children in Hawaii (she was a widow when they married) he contributed to their future success in many elective political offices. Wilson lived through tremendous social and political changes in California.

WILSON, MILBURN LINCOLN

218. McDean, Harry C. M. L. WILSON AND THE ORIGINS OF FEDERAL FARM POLICY IN THE GREAT PLAINS, 1909-1914.
Montana 1984 34(4): 50-59.

Milburn Lincoln Wilson joined the homestead rush to Montana in 1909. With a degree in agriculture, he believed he was well prepared to farm on the Montana plains. He failed his first year and acknowledged that farming by individual effort on the plains led to disaster. In 1911, Wilson became superintendent of 20 demonstration farms for the Montana Agricultural Experiment Station. Crop failures on these farms convinced him that eastern Montana's future was with livestock rather than cash crops. When Wilson became undersecretary of agriculture and a major architect of New Deal agricultural policy in the 1930's, his eastern Montana experience was a major influence on his ideas and proposals.

WOOD, STANLEY

219. Kedro, M. James. STANLEY WOOD, THE LITERARY ARTIST AS WESTERN PROMOTER.
Red River Valley Hist. Rev. 1975 11(3): 393-411.

Stanley Wood, a journalist and author, provided impetus to migrate west through his descriptive works; examines his work on the *Great Divide,* a literary journal of the West, 1889-96, and his career as a representative of a literary genre.

WOODHAMS, WILLIAM H.

220. Martin, Charles W., ed. THE DIARY OF WILLIAM H. WOODHAMS, 1852-1854: THE GREAT DESERTS OR AROUND AND ACROSS.
Nebraska Hist. 1980 61(1): 1-101.

William H. Woodhams (1829-91) started his diary on a sea voyage to California on 24 October 1852. He arrived in San Francisco on 11 March 1853. On 16 December 1853, along with his cousin, Woodhams started the return journey to his family homestead on the Kalamazoo River about 12 miles north of the city of Kalamazoo. They returned by way of Nicaragua and New York with a stopover in Troy, New York, and arrived home in Michigan on 5 February 1854. On 8 March 1854 he was off again to California, this time with horses to sell. Traveling the overland route, Woodhams reached the California gold fields at Elizabethtown on 22 July 1854. On 9 February 1855, he embarked in San Francisco for home. He arrived in New York on 5 March, and there his diary ends. The diary is important because it encompasses both sea and land voyages to California. The sea voyages include journeys round Cape Horn and across Nicaragua. The overland journey in 1854 followed the Beckwith route in California and provides one of the few descriptions of this variant of the California trail.

WOODWARD, THOMAS SIMPSON

221. Reid, Patsy Ruth. GENERAL THOMAS S. WOODWARD, SOUTHERN FRONTIERSMAN: THE WINN PARISH YEARS.
North Louisiana Hist. Assoc. J. 1980 11(1): 1-7.

Thomas Simpson Woodward (1794-1859) moved to Winn Parish, Louisiana, in 1853, where he farmed, growing cotton as his main crop. He owned 100 slaves and at the time of his death was one of the wealthiest men in northern Louisiana. His letters of reminiscences contain information about the tradition and history of the areas in which he had lived.

WRIGHT, ELIZUR (FAMILY)

222. French, David. PURITAN CONSERVATISM AND THE FRONTIER: THE ELIZUR WRIGHT FAMILY ON THE CONNECTICUT WESTERN RESERVE.
Old Northwest 1975 1(1): 85-95.

Elizur Wright I and his Yale-educated son, Elizur II, built pioneer farms: the father in wilderness Canaan, Connecticut; the son in the Western Reserve. Both were orthodox congregationalists, scientists, and mathematicians. In the next generation, Elizur III's study of science led to his questioning Puritan orthodoxy. Elizur II became a conservative religious leader and educator at Tallmadge, Ohio, but his son Elizur III returned to Connecticut to enter Yale University, representing the first generation to return east. Elizur III succeeded at Yale but abandoned the orthodoxy of his heritage. He became a follower of the agnostic Robert Ingersoll (1833-99).

WRIGHT, HAROLD BELL

223. Tagg, Lawrence V. A DEDICATION TO THE MEMORY OF HAROLD BELL WRIGHT, 1872-1944. *Arizona and the West 1980 22(4): 302-306.*

Harold Bell Wright (1872-1944) was born into a New York family whose poverty kept it on the move westward. After two years in the preparatory school of Hiram College in Ohio, his uncertain health forced him to quit. He worked for a few years as a farm laborer and preached in the Missouri Ozark Mountains. Discovering a flair for writing, he spent the remaining four decades of his life in California and Arizona. Wright had phenomenal success. Twelve novels were best-sellers, eight became movies, and sales totaled over 10 million. Although his critics pronounced his books literary disasters, his readers embraced their Social Gospel of democratic ideals and optimism. He looked upon his work as a "ministry of print."

Y

YOUNG, ANNA DURKEE TAUZIN

224. Curran, Nathaniel B. ANNA DURKEE TAUZIN YOUNG, 1753-1839: CONNECTICUT LADY, ILLINOIS PIONEER. *J. of the Illinois State Hist. Soc. 1984 77(2): 94-100.*

The daughter of a participant in the French and Indian, Pennamite, and Revolutionary wars, Anna Durkee was born in Connecticut. Her first husband was Dominic Tauzin, a physician in Lafayette's entourage, who drowned in a hurricane. She later married Norwich attorney John Young, but was widowed a second time in 1805. She migrated to Philadelphia in 1810 and to Brooklyn five years later. In 1817, she was in the first party of settlers at Hamel Township, Madison County, Illinois.

YOUNG, BRIGHAM

225. Jessee, Dean C. BRIGHAM YOUNG'S FAMILY: THE WILDERNESS YEARS.
Brigham Young U. Studies 1979 19(4): 474-500.

An account of the trials and tribulations of the family of Brigham Young during the Mormon migration from Nauvoo, Illinois, to Salt Lake City, Utah. Young already had numerous wives; the time, energy, and thought-consuming problems connected with directing the migration while simultaneously establishing a new home in the West left little time for his family. The wives and children did not leave as a unit, and several returned to Nauvoo or went from camp to camp. Their sufferings, faith, and efforts to communicate with their husband are carefully detailed.

226. Shipps, Jan. BRIGHAM YOUNG AND HIS TIMES: A CONTINUING FORCE IN MORMONISM.
Journal of the West 1984 23(1): 48-54.

Examines the 30-year career of "Brother Brigham" for reasons why the pioneer-politician-patriach outshone his predecessor, Joseph Smith. Two common assumptions—that the death of Joseph Smith unified the Saints and that a majority of Mormons left Nauvoo, Illinois, for Utah—are challenged. The trek to the Great Salt Lake Valley and the period during which the Kingdom of Zion was being built up are identified as the opportunities over which Young exercised his extraordinary leadership and established his influence, which persists to the present.

SUBJECT INDEX

Each biographical summary in this book is indexed below with a group (or "string") of index terms. Each of the terms in these strings will move around to the first or leading position in the string so that the entire index string will appear in the subject index as many times as there are terms in the string. This way, there are several different ways to access each biographical summary.

Each of the index strings appears in alphabetical order according to the leading term in bold. If a leading term is exactly the same as the leading term of the string preceding it, then it is replaced by a dash.

The final term in the string is a number in italics; this number refers to the number of the entry, not the page number on which the entry appears. The dates that precede the italicized entry number are the dates of the time period covered by the biographical article.

C_____

and Pioneer Life. Ohio.
Western Reserve. Yale
University. 1762-1870. *222*

**Connecticut (Hartford
County).** Captivity narratives.
Childbirth. Death and Dying.
King Philip's War.
Massachusetts (Lancaster).
1637-1711. *155*

Connecticut (Norwich).
Illinois. Pioneers. 1753-1839.
224

Construction. Copper Mines
and Mining. Investments.
Utah (Salt Lake City). Weir,
Thomas. 1879-1930. *128*

Converts. Congregationalism.
Family. Missions and
Missionaries. Vermont. 1789-
1819. *36*

Copper Mines and Mining.
Construction. Investments.
Utah (Salt Lake City). Weir,
Thomas. 1879-1930. *128*

Country Life. Anderson, Mary.
City Life. District of
Columbia. Farmers. Letters.
Maryland (Rockville area).
1854-1960. *8*

—. Basque Americans. Montana
(Valley County). Sheep
Raising. 1912-78. *76*

—. Civil War. Mississippi
(Pontotoc County). Personal
Narratives. 1864-69. *174*

Courtship. Wyoming
(Cheyenne). 1871-1910. *114*

Cowboys. Authors. Cattle
drives. Great Plains.
Southwest. 19c-1935. *1*

—. California, northern. Rodeos
(bronc busters). 1910's-25. *4*

—. Diaries. Frontier and Pioneer
Life. 1894. *62*

Criminals. Texas. 1851-78. *25*

D

Daily life. Account books.
Boardinghouses. Diaries.
Hannah Crowninshield House.
Inventories. Massachusetts
(Salem). 1791-1819. *32*

—. Alaska (Nome). Gold
Rushes. Personal Narratives.
1900-06. *86*

—. Alberta (Peace River area).
Personal Narratives. 1928-48.
19

—. California (Glendora).
Diaries. Women. 1885-1946.
195

—. Colorado. 1878-1937. *176*

—. Homesteading and
Homesteaders. Oklahoma
(Perry). Women. 1893-95.
118

—. Letters. Missionaries.
Oregon. 1840-80. *142*

—. Marriage. 1864-76. *60*

—. Oregon. Personal Narratives.
1899-1935. *56*

Danish Americans. California.
Frontier and Pioneer Life.
1800-59. *106*

Death. Bancroft, Edward. 1781-
89. *64*

Death. Captivity narratives.
Childbirth. Connecticut

—. Military Camps and Forts. North Dakota. Personal Narratives. South Dakota. 1866-70. *208*

—. New Mexico (Pecos Valley). Personal narratives. 1885-1895. *201*

Frontiersmen. 1756-1820. *38*

—. Folklore. Keelboatmen. 1790's-1820's. *78,79*

Fur trade. Alaska. Canada. Hudson's Bay Company. Russian-American Company. 1834-45. *171*

—. American Fur Company. Fort Laramie Treaty (1851). Indian Affairs, Superintendent of. Missouri River. 1828-61. *124*

—. American Fur Company. Frontier and Pioneer Life. Wisconsin (Green Bay). 1790-1846. *108*

—. Canada. Hudson's Bay Company. North West Company. 1808-58. *34*

—. Economic Conditions. Great Lakes. Social mobility. Women. 1775-1855. *163*

—. Entrepreneurs. 1808-47. *14*

Fur Traders. Frontier and Pioneer Life. Indian Agents. Indiana. 1800-55. *53*

—. Ontario (Lac Seul). 1803-54. *122*

G

Gardens. Botanists. Europe. Pennsylvania (Philadelphia). 1699-1777. *23*

Geography. Canada. Hudson's Bay Company. Societies (influence of). 1750-1800. *210*

Geology. Gold. Nova Scotia. Prospectors. 1857-63. *47*

Georgia. Children. Education. Explorers. Virginia. 1774-91. *110*

—. Indians, Cherokee. Leaders. Oklahoma. Removal, forced. Tennessee. 1815-66. *154*

—. Oklahoma. Presbyterian Church. 1820's-81. *84*

Georgia (Augusta; St. Paul's Parish). American Revolution. Church of England. Loyalists. 1775-83. *166*

Georgia (Savannah). American Revolution. Commerce. Jews. Memoirs. 1739-1809. *167*

German Americans. Catholic Church. Settlement. Texas, northwestern. 1891-1922. *149*

German Canadians. American Revolution. Diaries. Mercenary Soldiers. Military Service. 1776-83. *31*

German-Russian Americans. Frontier and Pioneer Life. North Dakota (McIntosh County). 1885-1910. *27*

Glacier National Park. Prairie Provinces. Trapping. 1890's-1944. *57*

Diaries. Inventories. Massachusetts (Salem). 1791-1819. *32*

Hanson, George A. American Revolution. Congress. Maryland. Swedish Americans. 18c. 1876. *95*

Hawaii. Missionaries. Protestants. 1820-1975. *37*

Hebard, Grace Raymond. Historiography. Lewis and Clark Expedition. Porivo. Waldo, Anna Lee. 1804-1980. *160*

Hedonism. Indian-White Relations. Massachusetts. Merry Mount (settlement). Plymouth Plantation. 1622-46. *125*

Historians. Illinois (Bishop Hill). Preservation. 1875-1919. *187*

Historiography. Hebard, Grace Raymond. Lewis and Clark Expedition. Porivo. Waldo, Anna Lee. 1804-1980. *160*

Homesteaders. Daily Life. Oklahoma (Perry). Women. 1893-95. *118*

—. Memoirs. Oregon. 1889-99. *55*

—. Oklahoma (Peggs, Sand Springs, Tahlequah). 1895-1937. *66*

—. Retail Trade. Washington (Marcus). 1862-1901. *133*

Hudson's Bay Company. Alaska. Canada. Fur trade. Russian-American Company. 1834-45. *171*

—. British Columbia (New Caledonia). Fort St. James. Indians, Carrier. Traders. 1780-1840. *105*

—. Canada. Fur trade. North West Company. 1808-58. *34*

—. Canada. Geography. Societies (influence of). 1750-1800. *210*

—. Indians, Metis. Manitoba. Provincial Government. 1853-79. *121*

—. Labrador. Letters. Quebec. Simpson, George. 1830's-50's. *175*

Hunting. Buffalo. Frontier and Pioneer Life. Manuscripts. 1868-80. *52*

Hunting, big game. Fort Hays. Kansas. 1869-70. *61*

I_____

Idaho. Bunker Hill and Sullivan Mine. Businessmen. Investors. 1887-92. *146*

—. Public Relations. Railroads. Strahorn, Robert Edmund. Washington (Spokane). Women. 1877-1925. *189*

Illinois. Connecticut (Norwich). Pioneers. 1753-1839. *224*

—. Indians (captivities). Miami Indians. 1784-1812. *212*

Illinois (Bishop Hill). Historians. Preservation. 1875-1919. *187*

Illinois (Nauvoo). Migration, Internal. Mormons. Utah (Salt Lake City). 1841-48. *225*

Indians, Metis. Hudson's Bay Company. Manitoba. Provincial Government. 1853-79. *121*

Indians, Miami. Wells, William. Wisconsin. 1780-1812. *112*

Indians (reservations). Cheyenne Indians (Northern). Montana. Murder. 1856-1904. *113*

Indian-White Relations. Cherokee Indians. Frontier and Pioneer Life. Military. Politics. Tennessee. Texas. 1807-63. *102*

—. Hedonism. Massachusetts. Merry Mount (settlement). Plymouth Plantation. 1622-46. *125*

—. Louisiana Territory, Upper. Osage Indians. Westward movement. 1804-18. *48*

—. Methodist Church. Missions and Missionaries. Wisconsin. 1793-1883. *42*

International Trade. California. Land. 1798-1886. *217*

Inventories. Account books. Boardinghouses. Daily life. Diaries. Hannah Crowninshield House. Massachusetts (Salem). 1791-1819. *32*

Investments. Construction. Copper Mines and Mining. Utah (Salt Lake City). Weir, Thomas. 1879-1930. *128*

Investors. Bunker Hill and Sullivan Mine. Businessmen. Idaho. 1887-92. *146*

Iowa (Story County; Ames). Law Enforcement. 1896-1922. *152*

Iowa, University of. Frontier and Pioneer Life. Immigrants. Psychology. Swedish Americans. ca 1869-1949. *165*

Iron Industry. Tennessee. Tunnels. ca 1790-1855. *28*

J

Jefferson, Thomas. American Revolution. Calvinists. Clergy. 1775-1808. *111*

—. Explorers. Lewis and Clark Expedition. Western States. 1803-06. *109*

Jews. American Revolution. Commerce. Georgia (Savannah). Memoirs. 1739-1809. *167*

—. Business. California (Pomona Valley). Ranching. 1848-1900. *136*

—. Colorado (Denver). Physicians. 1866-1922. *74*

—. North Dakota (Grand Forks). Rabbis. 1890-1934. *134*

Journalism. Abolition Movement. Feminism. Lowry, Sylvanus B. Minnesota. 1815-84. *196*

—. *Great Divide.* Literature (promotional). Westward Movement. 1879-96. *219*

Minnesota. Abolition Movement. Feminism. Journalism. Lowry, Sylvanus B. 1815-84. *196*

Minnesota, northern. Diaries. Missionaries. Wisconsin. 1833-49. *75*

Missionaries. Daily Life. Letters. Oregon. 1840-80. *142*

—. Diaries. Minnesota, northern. Wisconsin. 1833-49. *75*

—. Hawaii. Protestants. 1820-1975. *37*

Missions and Missionaries. Clergy. Edwards, Jonathan. Evangelism. Great Awakening. 1742-1850's. *41*

—. Congregationalism. Converts. Family. Vermont. 1789-1819. *36*

—. Diaries. Kentucky. North Central States. Presbyterian Church. 1828-45. *144*

—. Indian-White Relations. Methodist Church. Wisconsin. 1793-1883. *42*

—. Mississippi (Mayhew Mission). Oklahoma, southeastern. 1820-68. *43*

Mission-Thule Consolidated Agency. California. Collectors. Indian agents. 1889-1906. *159*

Mississippi (Mayhew Mission). Missions and Missionaries. Oklahoma, southeastern. 1820-68. *43*

Mississippi (Pontotoc County). Civil War. Country Life. Personal Narratives. 1864-69. *174*

Mississippi Valley, Upper. Explorers. 1818-32. *164*

Missouri Mounted Rangers. Armies. Frontier and Pioneer Life. 1799-1853. *40*

Missouri River. American Fur Company. Fort Laramie Treaty (1851). Fur trade. Indian Affairs, Superintendent of. 1828-61. *124*

Missouri (St. Louis). 1806-33. *51*

—. Chouteau, Auguste. Indian agents. Lewis and Clark expedition. Osage Indians. Travel. 1803-06. *49*

Missouri (St. Louis area). Boosterism. Frontier and Pioneer Life. Land. Local Government. Speculation. 1815-46. *138*

Montana. Businessmen. Cattle Ranchers. Sheep Ranchers. 1864-1937. *170*

—. Cheyenne Indians (Northern). Indians (reservations). Murder. 1856-1904. *113*

—. Christie, David. Fergus, James. Frontier and Pioneer Life. Letters. Women. 1860-85. *50*

—. Friendship. 1880-1925. *100*

—. Land grants. Metis. Race. Settlement. 1870-84. *153*

O

Indians, Metis. Manitoba. 1853-79. *121*

Psychology. Frontier and Pioneer Life. Immigrants. Iowa, University of. Swedish Americans. ca 1869-1949. *165*

Public Relations. Idaho. Railroads. Strahorn, Robert Edmund. Washington (Spokane). Women. 1877-1925. *189*

Q

Quebec. Hudson's Bay Company. Labrador. Letters. Simpson, George. 1830's-50's. *175*

Quinault Indian Agency. Pioneer life. Washington Territory. 1854-1937. *73*

R

Rabbis. Jews. North Dakota (Grand Forks). 1890-1934. *134*

Race. Land grants. Metis. Montana. Settlement. 1870-84. *153*

Railroads. Alberta (Crowsnest Pass). Robbery. 1920-24. *5*

—. Idaho. Public Relations. Strahorn, Robert Edmund. Washington (Spokane). Women. 1877-1925. *189*

Ranchers. Arizona. New Mexico. ca 1850-1917. *54*

—. Oregon (Grant County). Personal narratives. Rural life. 1870's-1947. *214*

Ranching. Business. California (Pomona Valley). Jews. 1848-1900. *136*

—. Diaries. Merchants. Wyoming (Cheyenne area). 1857-69. *213*

Rancho Camulos. California. Mexican Americans. Upper Classes. 1839-1938. *65*

Rattlesnakes. Alberta. Blackfoot Indians (Blood). 1844-1901. *45*

Real Estate Business. Agriculture. Settlement. Texas Panhandle. 1905-43. *180*

Rebellions. Texas (San Antonio de Bexar). Wales (Newport). 1835-40. *147*

Reform (movements). Metropolitan Protective Association. New Mexico (Santa Fe). New York City. 1875-1943. *183*

Reindeer. Alaska (Sinuk River). Eskimos. 1890-1907. *13*

Religion. Pennsylvania. Personality. Settlement. 1660-1700. *135*

Removal, forced. Georgia. Indians, Cherokee. Leaders. Oklahoma. Tennessee. 1815-66. *154*

Removals, forced. Indians, Cherokee. Political Factions. 1815-46. *185*

Republican Party. Banking. Kansas (Medicine Lodge). Oklahoma (Guthrie, Tulsa). 1873-1918. *123*

—. Frontier and Pioneer Life. Immigrants. Iowa, University of. Psychology. ca 1869-1949. *165*

T_____

Teaching. Alaska (Sitka). Attitudes. Frontier and Pioneer Life. Letters. 1888. *68*

—. Alberta College. Botany. Canada. Explorers. 1850-1920. *116*

Temperance Workers. Oklahoma. 1867-1911. *127*

Tennessee. Arkansas. Diplomats. Fort Campo de la Esperanza. Fort San Fernando. Spain. 1782-1823. *82*

—. Cherokee Indians. Frontier and Pioneer Life. Indian-White Relations. Military. Politics. Texas. 1807-63. *102*

—. Cherokee Indians. Indian Wars. Virginia. 1770's-94. *29*

—. Georgia. Indians, Cherokee. Leaders. Oklahoma. Removal, forced. 1815-66. *154*

—. Iron Industry. Tunnels. ca 1790-1855. *28*

Tennessee, middle. Settlement. 1703-1812. *99*

Texas. Arkansas (Fayetteville). California. Confederate Army. Indian Territory. Mexican War. 1845-65. *141*

—. California. Pioneers. Women. 1830-93. *150*

—. Cherokee Indians. Frontier and Pioneer Life. Indian-White

Relations. Military. Politics. Tennessee. 1807-63. *102*

—. Criminals. 1851-78. *25*

Texas, northwestern. Catholic Church. German Americans. Settlement. 1891-1922. *149*

Texas Panhandle. Agriculture. Real Estate Business. Settlement. 1905-43. *180*

Texas (San Antonio de Bexar). Rebellions. Wales (Newport). 1835-40. *147*

Texas (Waco). Merchants. Pioneers. Trade. 1830-83. *20*

Trade. Frontier and Pioneer Life. Great Plains. 1857-1904. *177*

—. Merchants. Pioneers. Texas (Waco). 1830-83. *20*

Trade Routes. Canada. Discovery and Exploration. Overland Journeys to the Pacific. 1789-93. *115*

Traders. British Columbia (New Caledonia). Fort St. James. Hudson's Bay Company. Indians, Carrier. 1780-1840. *105*

Trading post. Arizona. 1883-1977. *63*

Traitors. Letters. South Carolina. 1708. *126*

Trapping. Glacier National Park. Prairie Provinces. 1890's-1944. *57*

Travel. California. Gold Rushes. 1848-50. *26*

—. Chouteau, Auguste. Indian agents. Lewis and Clark expedition. Missouri (St. Louis). Osage Indians. 1803-06. *49*

Tunnels. Iron Industry. Tennessee. ca 1790-1855. *28*

Twin Territories. Editors. Five Civilized Tribes. Indians, Cherokee. Oklahoma. 1898-1904. *145*

U_____

Upper Classes. California. Mexican Americans. Rancho Camulos. 1839-1938. *65*

—. Code of honor. Flemming, Samuel (death). North Carolina (Morganton). 1851. *16*

Utah. Development. Philanthropy. 1903-20. *173*

Utah (Salt Lake City). Construction. Copper Mines and Mining. Investments. Weir, Thomas. 1879-1930. *128*

—. Illinois (Nauvoo). Migration, Internal. Mormons. 1841-48. *225*

Utah (Uinta Basin). Mormons. Philanthropy. Settlement. 1862-1937. *172*

V_____

Vermont. American Revolution. Authors. Orators. Soldiers. 1738-89. *6*

—. Congregationalism. Converts. Family. Missions and Missionaries. 1789-1819. *36*

Virginia. Business. Plantations. 1801-51. *87*

—. Cherokee Indians. Indian Wars. Tennessee. 1770's-94. *29*

—. Children. Education. Explorers. Georgia. 1774-91. *110*

—. Commerce. Plantations. Slavery. 1800-76. *88*

—. Economic Development. 1694-1744. *44*

—. Frontier and Pioneer Life. Military. Politics. 1770-1800. *46*

Virginia (Charles City County). Confessions. Murderers. Servants. Williams, Paul. 1650-70. *97*

Virginia (Norfolk). France. Great Britain. Navies. 1771-1818. *21*

Viticulture. California (San Gabriel Valley). Entrepreneurs. Settlement. Wilson, Benjamin D. 1860's-96. *169*

Voyages. California. Diaries. Gold Rushes. Overland Journeys to the Pacific. 1852-55. *220*

W_____

Waldo, Anna Lee. Hebard, Grace Raymond.

AUTHOR INDEX

LIST OF PERIODICALS

Alabama Review

Alaska Journal

Alberta History

American History Illustrated

American West

Annals of Iowa

Annals of Wyoming

Arizona and the West

BC Studies

Beaver

Brigham Young University Studies

Bulletin of the Board of Celtic Studies

California History

Canadian Ethnic Studies

Canadian Geographic

Chronicles of Oklahoma

Colorado Heritage

Colorado Magazine

Concordia Historical Institute
Quarterly

Daughters of the American Revolution
Magazine

Delaware History

Dialogue: A Journal of Mormon
Thought

Early American Literature

Essex Institute Historical Collections

Filson Club History Quarterly

Florida Historical Quarterly

Gateway Heritage

Hawaiian Journal of History

Historical Magazine of the Protestant
Episcopal Church

Historical New Hampshire

History Today

Idaho Yesterdays

Indiana Magazine of History

Inland Seas

Journal of Arizona History

Journal of Cherokee Studies

Journal of Mississippi History

Journal of Presbyterian History (now
American Presbyterians)

Journal of the Illinois State Historical
Society (now Illinois Historical Journal)

Journal of the Early Republic

Journal of the West

Kansas Historical Quarterly

Kansas History

Library Quarterly

Maine Historical Society Quarterly

Maryland Historical Magazine

Methodist History

Michael: On the History of the Jews in
the Diaspora

Michigan History

Minnesota History

Missouri Historical Review

Missouri Historical Society Bulletin
(superseded by Gateway Heritage)

Montana

Nebraska History

New England Historical and
Genealogical Register

New England Quarterly

New Mexico Historical Review

New York History

New-England Galaxy

North Carolina Historical Review

North Dakota History

North Louisiana Historical Association
Journal

Norwegian-American Studies

Nova Scotia Historical Quarterly (now
Nova Scotia Historical Review)

Old Northwest

Ontario History

Oregon Historical Quarterly

Pacific Historian

Pacific Northwest Quarterly

Pacific Northwesterner

Panhandle-Plains Historical Review

Pennsylvania Heritage

Pharmacy in History

Phylon

Proceedings of the American
Philosophical Society

Psychohistory Review

Red River Valley Historical Review

Register of the Kentucky Historical
Society

Smithsonian

Southern California Quarterly

Southern Studies

Swedish Pioneer Historical Quarterly

Swedish-American Historical Quarterly

Tennessee Historical Quarterly

Tequesta

Texana

Timeline

Utah Historical Quarterly

Virginia Cavalcade

Virginia Magazine of History and
Biography

Welsh History Review

West Tennessee Historical Society
Papers

Western States Jewish Historical
Quarterly

Western States Jewish History

William and Mary Quarterly

Wisconsin Magazine of History